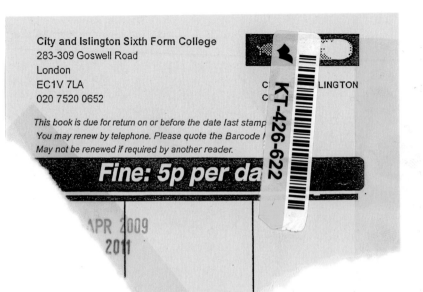

By the same author

*Classical Music: The Era of Haydn, Mozart, and Beethoven*

The Norton Introduction to Music History

# Anthology of
# CLASSICAL MUSIC

## EDITED BY PHILIP G. DOWNS

*The University of Western Ontario*

W • W • NORTON & COMPANY

*New York • London*

The text of this book is composed in Bembo.

Library of Congress Cataloguing-in-Publication Data

Anthology of classical music / edited by Philip G. Downs.
   p. of music. — (The Norton introduction to music history)
   Vocal portions with French, German, Italian, or Latin words.
   Intended for use with the editor's Classical music.
   1. Musical appreciation—Music collections.   2. Musical analysis—
Music collections.   3. Music—18th century.   4. Music—19th century.
I. Downs, Philip G.   II. Downs, Philip G.   Classical music.   III. Series.
MT6.5.A56    1992                                    92-17717

ISBN 0-393-95209-6

W. W. Norton & Company, Inc.
500 Fifth Avenue, New York, N.Y. 10110
W. W. Norton & Company. Ltd.
10 Coptic Street, London WC1A 1PU

4 5 6 7 8 9

# Contents

# Preface

Every anthology is the result of a series of choices, and in the case of the *Anthology of Classical Music* those choices were governed largely by the shape of the companion volume, *Classical Music: The Era of Haydn, Mozart, and Beethoven,* published by W. W. Norton in their series, *Introduction to Music History.* There, it was decided that in addition to examining the "great masters" thoroughly, the book should also include as extensive an exploration of lesser composers of the period as possible; so it was clear that this anthology should also reflect that policy.

Over the last few decades the widespread availability of well-known masterworks (e.g. Mozart's 40th Symphony, or Beethoven's Fifth) in anthologies and study scores have made it seem advisable to refrain from providing yet another printing of the same works, however important. I thought it more useful here to offer the reader a wider selection of relatively unknown compositions, some of obvious musical excellence, and a few of only sociological interest, in addition to the carefully pondered, representative works of the great masters. It is hoped that the inclusion of examples of musical ephemera will add depth and perspective to the broader picture of the musical life of the eighteenth century.

The value of taking a score to the piano and becoming acquainted with the musical artwork through the fingers, as well as the ears and eyes, is well known. Yet, it is only the truly exceptional musician who can read a large orchestral score with facility. For this reason a large proportion of the anthology consists of compositions on two or three staves. It is hoped that such works, illustrating the historical or compositional principles of the time, will also serve as subjects for analysis, for orchestration, or for other uses, and at the same time will invite the student to the keyboard in order to enjoy the music. Many eighteenth-century publications of music were designed to serve the multiple purpose of developing taste and ability in ornamentation, developing finger dexterity, and gaining insight into the processes of composition. It is my hope that this anthology may serve a similar purpose.

For constant patience and unfailing help, I wish to thank Claire Brook—one of the wisest people I know, whose wisdom is matched by her experience and whose humanity surely exceeds both, and Suzanne La Plante, her assistant, whose efficiency and humor saw the work through all its complex steps to completion. What a team!

All translations that follow the musical excerpts are by the editor unless otherwise stated.

# 1

GIUSEPPE TARTINI (1692–1770)
*Violin Sonata*, Opus 1, No. 4 (1734), first
movement

**2**

CARL PHILIPP EMANUEL BACH (1714–88)
*Trio Sonata in B♭ Major*, H.578, W.161/2
(1748), first movement

# 3

## JOHANN STAMITZ (1717–57)
### *Six Sonates à trois ou avec tout l'orchestre*, Opus 1, No. 1 (1755), first movement

# 4

## DOMENICO SCARLATTI (1685–1757)
*Sonata for Harpsichord in G Major, K.2 (1738)*

# 5

## D. SCARLATTI
### *Sonata for Harpsichord in D Major,* K.492 (1738)

# 6

## BALDASSARE GALUPPI (1706–85)
### *Sonata No. 2 for Harpsichord* (published 1756 by Walsh), first movement (toccata)

# 7

## JIŘI (GEORG) BENDA (1722–95)
*Sonata for Harpsichord in B♭ Major* (published 1757), first and second movements

# 8

## WILHELM FRIEDEMANN BACH (1710–84)
### *Polonaise No. 2 in C Minor (c. 1765)*

# 9

## C. P. E. BACH
*Sonata in D Minor*, H.5 (1732), first movement

# 10

## C. P. E. BACH
*Sonata in C Major,* H.46 (1746), first and second movements

### I

II

# 11

## GIOVANNI BATTISTA SAMMARTINI
## (1700/01–75)
## *Symphony No. 13* (published 1761)

### I

From *Harvard Publications in Music*, II, vol. 1: *The Early Symphonies*, ed. by Bathia Churgin. Cambridge, MA: Harvard University Press. © Copyright 1968 by the President and Fellows of Harvard College. Reprinted by permission.

## II

# III

# 12

STAMITZ
*Symphony in D Major (La Melodia Germanica,
No. 1) (c. 1754)*, first movement

# 13

PIETRO NARDINI (1722–93)
*Sonata in D Major for Violin and Basso Continuo*
(*Six sonates*, No. 2, printed in Venice, 1760),
first movement

# 14

GIOVANNI MARCO PLACIDO RUTINI
(1723–97)
*Sonata in F Major*, Opus 8, No. 1 (before 1774),
first movement

# 15

JOHANN SCHOBERT (*c.* 1735–67)
*Sonata for Keyboard with Optional Violin*, Opus 4,
No. 2 (before 1767), first movement

# 16

C. P. E. BACH
*Sonata in B Minor "für Kenner und Liebhaber,"*
H.245 (1774)

## I

II

Andante.

Fine.

# III

# 17

MUZIO CLEMENTI (1752–1832)
*Piano Sonata in A Major*, Opus 2, No. 4
(published 1779), second movement

# 18

## LUIGI BOCCHERINI (1743–1805)
*String Quartet*, Opus 2, No. 2, G.160 (1761)

# 19

## CARLO D'ORDONEZ (1734–86)
*String Quartet*, Opus 1, No. 1 (*c.* 1765), first
movement

From *Recent Researches in the Music of the Classical Era*, vol. 10. Copyright 1980 by A–R
Editions, Inc., Madison, WI. Reproduced by Permission.

# 20

JOHANN CHRISTIAN BACH (1735–82)
*Simphonie in E♭ Major,* Opus 6, No. 3 (before 1762), first movement

# 21

## C. P. E. BACH
*Sinfonie in D Major*, H.663 (1775/6), first and second movements

## I

**II**

# 22

## NICCOLÒ PICCINNI (1728–1800)
## *La buona figliuola* (1760), Act II, Scenes 12 and 13

Cecchina o La Buona Figliola. N. Piccinni, edited by G. Benvenuti. Reprinted by permission of G. Ricordi & C., SPA/Fondaziono Bravi. Hendon Music, Inc., Agents.

SCENA XIII. Il Marchese e Tagliaferro (osservando Cecchina
che dorme, sottovoce tra di loro).

*RECITATIVO*

**Scene 12**

**Cecchina**

| | |
|---|---|
| Vieni, il mio seno, | Come, my breast, |
| Di duol ripieno, | Full of grief, |
| Dolce riposo, | Sweet repose, |
| A consolar. | To console. |

*(She falls asleep.)*

## Scene 13

### The Marquis and Tagliaferro

*(looking at Cecchina asleep, whispering to each other.)*

**Marquis**

Ecco, dorme Cecchina.

Look, Cecchina is asleep.

**Tagliaferro**

Pofera piclina.

Poor li'l thing.

**Marquis**

Già sapete tutto quel che ha passato:
Ogni travaglio suo già vi ho narrato.
Lasciamola dormire.

You know everything that has happened: I have already told you about all her troubles. Let's let her sleep.

**Tagliaferro**

Jò, main Schatz.

Yes, my treasure.

**Marquis**

Quand'ella si risvegli tutto da me
saprà. Voglio al fattore parlare intanto,
perché pronto e lesto, sia per le nozze
mie. Ritorno presto: Senza di me, vi
prego non parlar. Voglio esser pre-
sente alla sorpresa sua. Ritornerò. Mi
raccomando.

When she wakes up, I'll tell her everything. I shall go and speak to the
steward directly, so that all may be
quickly made ready for my wedding.
I'll return at once. Please don't speak
to her while I'm away. I want to be
present to see her surprise. Goodbye.

**Tagliaferro**

Jò.

Yes.

**Marquis**

Giubilo di contento. Addio, monsieur.

I am bursting with happiness. Farewell,
monsieur.

**Tagliaferro** *(angry)*

Du bist ain Narr.

You are a fool.

**Marquis**

No, non lo dirò più.

No, I'll say no more.

# 23

## CHRISTOPH WILLIBALD GLUCK
## (1714–87)
### *Orfeo ed Euridice* (1762), Act I, Scenes 1 and 2★

## Scene 1

★This is the Paris version of 1774. The French recitative here is shorter than the original Italian recitative.

## RÉCITATIF.

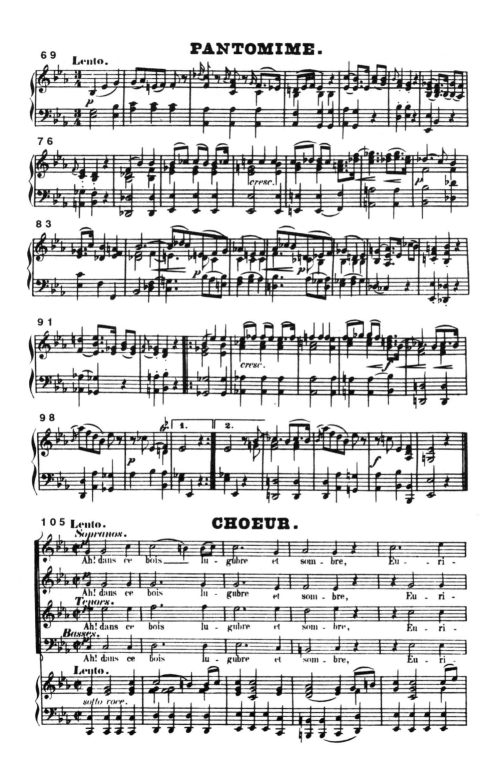

125

lar _ mes que pour toi l'on ré _ pand, que pour toi, que pour toi l'on ré _ pand.

lar _ mes que pour toi l'on ré _ pand, que pour toi, que pour toi l'on ré _ pand.

lar _ mes que pour toi l'on ré _ pand, vois les lar _ mes que pour toi l'on ré _ pand.

lar _ mes que pour toi l'on ré _ pand, vois les lar _ mes que pour toi l'on ré _ pand.

## RÉCITATIF.

132 ORPHÉE.

E _ loi _ gnez _ vous; ce lieu con _ vient à ma dou _

134

leur, et je veux sans té _ moins y ré _ pan _ dre des pleurs.

## RITOURNELLE.

Lento. 137

## Scene 2

### AIR.

**RÉCITATIF.**

## AIR.

## RÉCITATIF.

**100**

u-ne main tremblante. Echo. Eu-ri - di - ce n'est plus, et je res-pire en-

**105**

cor. Dieux, ren-dez _ lui la vi - e, ou don-nez-moi la mort! Echo.

**AIR.**

Andantino.

**110** ORPHÉE.

Plein de trouble et d'ef-froi, que de maux loin de toi,

**117**

mon coeur en - du - re, mon coeur en - du - re; Echo.

**125**

té - moins de mes mal - heurs, sen - si - ble à mes dou -

### Scene 1
#### Chorus

Ah! dans ce bois tranquille et sombre,
Euridice, si ton ombre nous entend . . .

Ah! In this dark and quiet wood,
Euridice, if your spirit hears us . . .

#### Orphée

Euridice!

Euridice!

#### Chorus

sois sensible à nos alarmes, vois nos peines.

Be aware of our fears, see our distress.

#### Soloists

Vois les larmes.

See our tears.

#### Chorus

Vois les larmes que pour toi l'on répand.

See the tears that are shed for you.

#### Orphée

Euridice!

Euridice!

#### Chorus

Ah! prends pitié du malheureux Orphée.

Ah, take pity on unhappy Orpheus.

#### Soloists

Il soupire, il gémit, il plaint sa destinée.

He sighs, he groans, he bemoans his fate.

#### Orphée

Euridice!

Euridice!

### Chorus

L'amoureuse tourterelle, toujours tendre, toujours fidèle, ainsi soupire et meurt de douleur.

The loving turtledove, ever gentle, ever faithful, sighs thus and dies of grief.

### Orphée: Recitative

Vos plaintes, vos regrets augmentent mon supplice! Aux mânes sacrés d'Euridice rendez les suprêmes honneurs, et couvrez son tombeau de fleurs.

Your moans, your sorrows increase my torture! Pay the highest tribute to the sacred shades of Euridice, and cover her tomb with flowers.

### Pantomime

### Chorus

Ah! dans ce bois lugubre et sombre, Euridice, si ton ombre nous entend, sois sensible à nos alarmes, vois nos peines, vois les larmes, que pour toi l'on répand, que pour toi l'on répand.

Ah, within this sad, dark wood, Euridice, if your spirit hears us, be aware of our fears, see our distress; see the tears that are shed for you, that are shed for you.

### Orphée: Recitative

Eloignez-vous; ce lieu convient à ma douleur, et je veux sans témoins y répandre des pleurs.

Leave me. This place is fitting for my grief, and I wish to weep here unobserved.

### Ritornello

### Scene 2
### Orphée: Air

Objet de mon amour,
Je te demande au jour
avant l'aurore,
avant l'aurore;
et quand le jour s'enfuit,
ma voix pendant la nuit,
t'appelle encore,
t'appelle encore,
t'appelle encore.

Object of my love,
By day I ask for you
Before dawn,
Before dawn;
And when the day is done
I still call for you at night
Still call for you,
Still call for you,
Still call for you.

### Orphée: Recitative

Euridice, Euridice, ombre chère, ah! dans quels lieux es-tu? Ton époux gémissant, interdit, éperdu, te demande sans cesse, à la nature entière les vents, hélas! emportent sa prière, emportent sa prière.

Euridice, Euridice, dear spirit, ah, where are you? Your groaning spouse, distracted, bewildered, asks for you unceasingly. The winds, alas, carry off his prayers to all creation.

### Orphée: Air

| | |
|---|---|
| Accablé de regrets, | Overwhelmed with sorrows, |
| je parcours des forêts | I pass through the forests, |
| la vaste enceinte, | the vast breadth, |
| la vaste enceinte. | the vast breadth. |
| Touché de mon destin | Touched by my fate, |
| l'écho répète en vain | The echo vainly repeats |
| ma triste plainte, | my sad complaint, |
| ma triste plainte, | my sad complaint, |
| ma triste plainte. | my sad complaint. |

### Orphée: Recitative

Euridice, Euridice! de ce doux nom tout retentit, ces bois, ces rochers, ce vallon. Sur les troncs dépouillés, sur l'écorce naissante on lit ce mot gravé par une main tremblante. Euridice n'est plus, et je respire encore. Dieux, rendez–lui la vie, ou donnez–moi la mort!

Euridice, Euridice, everything resounds with your sweet name, these woods, these rocks, this valley. On the stripped tree trunks, on the new-grown bark there is the word carved with a trembling hand. Euridice is no more, yet I still breathe. Gods, give her back her life or give me death!

### Orphée: Air

| | |
|---|---|
| Plein de trouble et d'effroi, | Full of distress and terror, |
| que de maux loin de toi, | how many evils far from you, |
| mon coeur endure, | my heart endures, |
| mon coeur endure; | my heart endures; |
| témoins de mes malheurs, | witnesses of my misery, |
| sensible à mes douleurs | sensible of my grief, |
| l'onde murmure, | the waves murmur, |
| l'onde murmure, | the waves murmur, |
| l'onde murmure. | the waves murmur. |

# 24

## BENDA
### *Ariadne auf Naxos* (1775), Scene

**Ariadne**

Sie? Ariadne? Sie, die Lust und Hoffnung
eines Königreichs! die Tochter Minos!
eines Gottes Enkelin, muß hier in ihres
Lebens Morgenröte, die Hände ringend
und verlassen, auf diesem Felsen irren? ein
Spott der Götter, ein Raub der Tiere sein?

You? Ariadne? She who was the joy and
the hope of a kingdom? the daughter of
Minos, granddaughter of a god, in the
dawn of her life, wandering among these
rocks, wringing her hands and abandoned?
an object of scorn to the Gods, to be the
prey of wild beasts?

\* Einst war ich schuldlos! Ohne Kummer,
ohne Tränen, heiter und froh blühte mein
Frühling, noch unbekannt der Liebe!

Once I was innocent. Free from grief, free
from tears, serene and happy was my
youth, knowing nothing yet of love.

130

* An meiner Mutter Busen ruhend, ihr
Stolz, ihr süßes Mädchen, von ihren
Küssen bedacht, von ihren Armen um–
schlungen, so, so entfloh sie mir, die beste,
goldne Zeit!

Resting on my mother's breast, her pride,
her sweet little girl, covered with her kisses,
enclosed in her arms; thus, thus that best,
that golden time has escaped from me.

* Kann nichts sie zurück erflehen?

Can nothing bring it back again?

** Bin ich ohne Rettung verloren?

Am I lost without hope of rescue?

* Durch einen einzigen Fehltritt verloren?

Lost because of one solitary mistake?

** Um eines einzigen Fehltritts willen von
Göttern und Menschen verstoßen?

Because of one offence against the gods and
men?

**504**

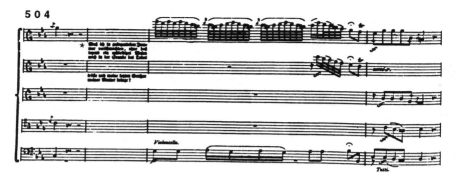

★ Muß ich in grenzlosem Jammer ver-
schmachten, ohne dass irgend ein mitlei-
diges Wesen mich in der Stunde des Todes
tröste und meine letzten Seufzer meiner
Mutter bringe?

Must I languish in endless lamentation with
no one to bring me comfort in the hour of
death and carry my last sighs to my
mother?

**507**

★ Könnt ich nur noch einmal zu deinen
Füssen sinken, o meine Mutter! in den
Staub gebeugt, noch einmal deine Füsse
mit meinen Tränen netzen.

If only I could once more sink at your feet,
oh, mother! and, bent down in the dust,
once more wash your feet with my tears!

** Kennst du mich nicht mehr, deine un-
dankbare, deine pflichtvergessene, deine
reuige Tochter? *(knieend)*

Do you no longer know your ungrateful,
undutiful, penitent daughter? *(kneeling)*

**510**

* Vergib ihr! Es ist so edel, so göttlich,
zu verzeihen! Vergib ihr! Er ist erfüllt, dein
Fluch! Nimm ihn zurück! Segne mich,
und lass mich sterben!

Forgive her! It is so noble, so godlike to
forgive! Forgive her! Your curse is fulfilled!
Take it back! Bless me, and let me die!

# 25

## JOSEPH HAYDN (1732–1809)
### *Sonata in G Major*, Hob. XVI:G1 (before 1760), first movement

# 26

HAYDN
*Sonata in G Minor,* Hob. XVI:44 (*c.* 1771/73),
first movement

# 27

HAYDN
*Sonata in A♭ Major,* Hob. XVI:46 (*c.* 1767/70),
second movement

# 28

## HAYDN
*Symphony No. 21 in A Major,* Hob. I:21 (1764),
first movement

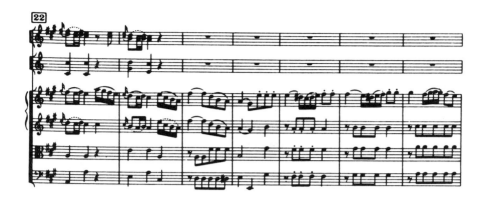

# 29

HAYDN
*Lo speziale*, Hob. XXVIII:3 (1768), Act III, No. 20: "Salamelica, Semprugna cara"

**No. 14 Aria**

**Volpino**

| | |
|---|---|
| Salamelica, Semprugna cara, | Salaamaleikum, noble Sempronio, |
| Constantinupola, – nupola, nupola, | Constantinople, – tinople, tinople, |
| Sempre cantara, sempre ballara, | Always singing, always dancing, |
| Dadl, dadl, dadl, dadl, dara | Diddle, diddle, diddle, diddle, dara |
| (etc.). | (etc.). |

# 30

HAYDN
*Sonata in A Major*, Hob. XVI:26 (1773), last movement

# 31

HAYDN
*String Quartet in Eb Major*, Opus 20, No. 1,
Hob. III:31 (1772), first and third movements

## I

# III

# 32

HAYDN
*Symphony No. 45 in F# Minor* ("Farewell"),
Hob. I:45 (1772), first movement

# 33

## HAYDN
*La vera costanza*, Hob.XXVIII:8 (1778?), Act II,
Finale★

★The German translation given here was the perferred version for performance at
the turn of the 19th century, under the title *Die wahre Beständigkeit.*

From Edition Peters No. 4999. Used by permission of C. F. Peters Corporation, New
York, NY.

### Villotto *(sneaks onstage; Lisetta behind him)*

Nimm dir ein Herz, Villotto!
Tapfer und ohne Schaudern
darfst du als Held nicht Zaudern,
bringe den Kerl jetzt um!
Ja, ohne lang zu zaudern,
bring' ich den Kerl jetzt um.
Nur frisch begonnen!
O Himmel—er regt sich,
er wacht gar auf—weh mir!
Pst! Stille! 's war ein Irrtum,
stille, ja, er schläft noch!
Drum frisch begonnen, vorwärts!

Get yourself a real heart, Villotto!
Bold and untrembling
As a hero you cannot delay,
Kill the fellow now!
Yes, without long hesitation
I'll kill the fellow straightaway.
Now to it!
O heavens—he's moving,
He's waking up—just my luck!
Shh! Quiet! that was a mistake,
Quiet! yes, he's asleep again!
So now to it, onwards!

### Lisetta

Masino, Achtung!

Masino, look out!

### Villotto

O weh—o weh!

Damnation!

### Masino

Was gibt's denn? Wer rief? Was ist los?

What's happening? Who called?
What's up?

### Masino, Villotto

Warum denn solch ein Geschrei? Wa–
rum, so sprich?

What's all the fuss about? What's going
on?

### Lisetta

Ich sollte wohl gar schweigen, wenn
hier ein Meuchelmörder 'nen
Schlafenden schön langsam ins Jenseits
bringen will.

I should keep quiet when this assassin
here is about to dispatch a sleeping
man at his leisure?

**Villotto**

Glaub' ihr kein Wort, sie lügt ja!      Don't believe a word of it. She's lying.

**Masino**

Ei, sieh an, welch ein Spässchen, dafür      Well, well, what a funny story, and I'll
erwürg' ich dich.      strangle you for it.

**Villotto**

Prahlhans, das wird sich zeigen.      Big talk! we'll see about that.

**Masino**

Wart' nur, gleich wirst du schweigen.      Wait a bit. You'll soon be shutting up.

**Lisetta**

O Himmel! Geht auseinander!      O heavens! Break it up!

**Masino, Villotto**

Gleich pakke dich von hier, du Schuft!      Get out of here, you worm!

**Villotto**

Später werd' ich dir's zeigen.      I'll teach you a lesson later on.

**Masino**

Wart' nur, gleich wirst du schweigen!      Hang on. I'll soon shut you up.

**Masino, Villotto**

Ich zittere und bebe,      I shiver and shake,
ich möcht' ihn massakrieren,      I would like to massacre him,
ich bin ganz außer mir.      I am quite beside myself.

**Lisetta**

Ich zittere und bebe,      I shiver and shake,
Er möcht' ihn massakrieren,      He would like to massacre him,
Er ist ganz außer sich.      He is quite beside himself.

# 34

## WOLFGANG AMADEUS MOZART
(1756–91)
*Andante in C Major* from "Nannerl's Music Book," K.1a (1761)

# 35

## MOZART
*Menuetto in F Major* from "Nannerl's Music Book," K.1d (1761)

# 36

## MOZART
*Keyboard Piece in G Minor* from the "London Notebook," K.15p (1764)

Nos. 34, 35, and 36 are from the *Neue Mozart Ausgabe*, Serie IX, Werkgruppe 27, Band 1, ed. by Wolfgang Plath. © 1982 by Bärenreiter-Verlag, Kassel. All Rights Reserved. Reprinted by Permission.

# 37

## MOZART
*Symphony No. 21 in A Major*, K.134 (1772), first movement

# 38

## MOZART
*String Quartet in F Major*, K.168 (1773), second movement

*Neue Mozart Ausgabe*, Serie VIII, Werkgruppe 20, Abteilung 1, Band 1, ed. by Karl Heinz Füssl, Wolfgang Plath, and Wolfgang Rehm. © 1966 by Bärenreiter-Verlag, Kassel. All Rights Reserved. Reprinted by Permission.

# 39

MOZART
*Sonata for Violin and Piano in E Minor, K.304*
(1778)

**151**

**159**

**165**

# 40

## MOZART
*Idomeneo*, K.366 (1781), Overture and Act I,
Scene 1

## Overture

## Act I, Scene 1

RECITATIVO

ILIA (alone)                              Andantino

Quando avran fi_ne o_ma_i    l'a_spre sventu_re  mi_e?

Ilia   in_fe_li_ce!        Di tem_pe_sta cru_del mi_se_ro a_

van_zo, del ge_ni_tor, e de' ger_ma_ni pri_va del bar_ba_ro ne_

### ARIA

*(Ilia's apartments in the royal palace. A gallery in the background.)*

## Scene 1 *(Ilia alone)*
### Recitativo

Quando avran fine omai l'aspre sventure mie? Ilia infelice! Di tempesta crudel misero avanzo, del genitor e de'germani priva del barbaro nemico misto col sangue il sangue vittime generose, a qual sorte più rea ti riserbano i Numi? . . . Pur vendicaste voi di Priamo e di Troia i danni e l'onte? Perì la flotta Argiva, e Idomeneo pasto forse sarà d'orca vorace . . . ma che mi giova, oh ciel! se al primo aspetto di quel prode Idamante, che all'onde mi rapì, l'odio deposi, e pria fu schiavo il cor, che m'accorgessi d'essere prigioniera. Ah qual contrasto, oh Dio! d'opposti affetti mi destate nel sen odio, ed amore! Vendetta deggio a chi mi diè la vita, gratitudine a chi vita mi rende . . . oh Ilia! oh genitor! oh prence! oh sorte! oh vita sventurata! oh dolce morte! Ma che? m'ama Idamante? . . . ah no; l'ingrato per Elettra sospira, e quell' Elettra meschina principessa, esule d'Argo, d'Oreste alle sciagure a queste arene fuggitiva, raminga, è mia rivale. Quanti mi siete intorno carnefici spietati? . . . orsù sbranate vendetta, gelosia, odio, ed amore, sbranate sì, sbranate sì quest'infelice core!

When will my cruel suffering ever end? Unhappy Ilia! The miserable survivor of the fierce storm, deprived of father and brothers, the blood of the barbarous enemy mingled with that of their noble victims, what evil fate have the gods reserved for you? . . . Did you even avenge Priam's and Troy's injuries and shame? The Greek fleet is destroyed and Idomeneo perhaps the food of a ravenous whale . . . but, Heavens, what's that to me? At the first glimpse of brave Idamante, who snatched me out of the water, I laid aside my hatred, and my heart was enslaved before I even realized I was a prisoner. Oh God! what feelings of love and hatred do you arouse within me! I owe vengence to him who gave me life, and gratitude to him who restored me to life . . . Oh Ilia! oh Father! oh prince! oh fate! oh unlucky life! ah sweet death! But does Idamante love me? No, he sighs for Electra, and she, wretched princess, exiled from Argos, arrived at these shores having fled the misfortunes of Orestes, is my rival. How many pitiless butchers surround me? Vendetta, jealousy, hatred, and love, tear apart this miserable heart.

### Aria

Padre, germani, addio!
Voi foste, io vi perdei.
Grecia, cagion tu sei.
E un greco adorerò?

Father, brothers, farewell!
Once you existed, I have lost you.
You, Greece, are the cause.
And shall I then love a Greek?

D'ingrata al sangue mio
So che la colpa avrei
Ma quel sembiante, oh Dei!
Odiare ancor non so.

Ungrateful to my own blood
I know that I would be guilty.
But, ye Gods! those features,
I cannot yet hate.

### Recitativo

Ecco, Idamante, ahimè! sen vien.
Misero core tu palpiti, e paventi. Deh cessate per poco, oh miei tormenti!

There is Idamante, alas! he is coming.
Miserable heart, you tremble in fear.
Cease, sufferings, if only for a little!

# 41

MOZART
*Vesperae solennes de confessore*, K.339 (1780),
"Laudate Dominum" (Psalm 117)

Laudate Dominum omnes gentes, laudate eum omnes populi. Quoniam confirmata est super nos misericordia ejus, et veritas Domini manet in aeternum. Gloria patri et filio et spiritui sancto, sicut erat in principio, et nunc et semper, et in saecula saeculorum. Amen.

O praise the Lord, all ye nations: praise him, all ye people. For his merciful kindness is great toward us: and the truth of the Lord endureth for ever. Glory be to the Father, and to the Son, and to the Holy Ghost, as it was in the beginning, is now, and ever shall be, world without end. Amen.

# 42

## C. P. E. BACH
*Sonata in D Major "für Kenner und Liebhaber,"*
H.286 (1785), first movement

*attacca*

# 43

C. P. E. BACH
*Sonata in C Minor*, H.298 (1786), first
movement

# 44

C. P. E. BACH
*Rondo in G Major "für Kenner und Liebhaber,"*
H.271 (1781)

# 45

JAN LADISLAV DUSSEK (1760–1812)
*Piano Sonata in G Major*, Opus 35, No. 2
(1797), first movement

# 46

CLEMENTI
*Piano Sonata in G Major*, Opus 37, No. 2 (1798),
first and second movements

# 47

JOSEF GELINEK (1758–1825)
*Variations on the Queen of Prussia's Favourite Waltz* (*c.* 1812), theme and variation no. 3

# 48

IGNACE JOSEPH PLEYEL (1757–1831)
*Six Sonatas for the Pianoforte or Harpsichord*, with optional flute, violin, and violoncello: No. 5 (1788), first movement

# 49

## JOHANN RUDOLF ZUMSTEEG
## (1760–1802)
## *Nachtgesang* (published 1800)

stil - ler, ihr Funkelnden, bei euch, als in der Ei - tel - kei - ten aufruhrvol - lem Reich?

| | |
|---|---|
| Tiefe Feyer | A deep rest |
| schauert um die Welt. | Falls over the world. |
| Braune Schleyer | A brown veil |
| hüllen Wald und Feld. | Covers wood and field. |
| Trüb und matt und müde | Dull and faint and tired, |
| nickt jedes Leben ein, | Everything that lives nods off, |
| und namenloser Friede | And a nameless peace |
| umsäuselt alles Seyn! | Whispers around every being. |
| | |
| Wacher Kummer, | Waking grief, |
| verlass ein Weilchen mich! | Leave me for a little while! |
| Goldener Schlummer, | Golden slumber |
| komm und umflügle mich! | Come and enfold me in your wings! |
| Trockne meine Thränen | Dry my tears |
| mit deines Schleyers Saum, | With the hem of your veil, |
| und tausche, Freund, mein Sehnen | And, Friend, exchange my longings |
| mit deinem schönsten Traum. | For your most beautiful dreaming. |
| | |
| Blaue Ferne, | Oh, blue distance, |
| hoch über mich erhöht! | Raised high above me! |
| Heilge Sterne, | Holy stars, |
| in hehrer Majestät! | In sublime majesty! |
| sagt mir, ist es stiller, | Tell me, is it more still, |
| ihr Funkelden, bei euch, | You bright ones, where you are |
| als in der Eitelkeiten | Than here in the kingdom |
| aufruhrvollem Reich? | Of vanity and tumult? |

# 50

## JOHANN FRIEDRICH REICHARDT
## (1752–1814)
### *Erlkönig* (published 1794)

Wer reitet so spät durch Nacht und
    Wind?
Es ist der Vater mit seinem Kind.
Er hat den Knaben wohl in dem Arm,
Er fasst ihn sicher, er hält ihn
    warm.

Mein Sohn, was birgst du so bang dein
    Gesicht?
Siehst, Vater, du den Erlkönig nicht?
Den Erlenkönig mit Kron' und
    Schweif?
Mein Sohn, es ist ein Nebelstreif.

"Du Liebes Kind, komm, geh mit mir;
Gar schöne Spiele spiel' ich mit dir.
Manch bunte Blumen sind an dem
    Strand,
Meine Mutter hat manch gülden
    Gewand."

Who rides so late thro' night and
    wind?
It is the father with his child.
He has the boy firm in his arm,
He holds him secure, he keeps him
    warm.

My son, why do you look so
    frightened?
Father, don't you see the Erlking?
The Erlking, with crown and
    train?
My son, it's a streak of mist.

"Come with me, you dear child;
I shall play wonderful games with you.
There are many colored flowers
    on the shore,
My mother has many golden
    dresses."

Mein Vater, mein Vater, und hörest du
  nicht,
Was Erlenkönig mir leise ver-
  spricht?
Sei ruhig; bleibe ruhig, mein Kind,
In dürren Blättern säuselt der Wind.

"Willst, feiner Knabe, du mit mir
  gehn?
Meine Töchter sollen dich warten
  schön,
Meine Töchter führen den nächtlichen
  Reihn,
Und wiegen und tanzen und singen
  dich ein."

Mein Vater, mein Vater, und siehst du
  nicht dort
Erlkönigs Töchter am düstern
  Ort?
Mein Sohn, mein Sohn, ich seh' es
  genau;
Es scheinen die alten Weiden so grau.

"Ich lieb' dich, mich reizt deine
  schöne Gestalt;
Und bist du nicht willig, so brauch' ich
  Gewalt."
Mein Vater, mein Vater, jetzt fasst er
  mich an!
Erlkönig hat mir ein Leids getan!

Dem Vater grauset's, er reitet
geschwind,
Er hält in Armen das ächzende
  Kind,
Erreicht den Hof mit Mühe und
  Not;
In seinen Armen das Kind war tot.

Father, father, do you not
  hear
What the Erlking is quietly
  promising me?
Be quiet; stay quiet, my child,
The wind is rustling in the dry leaves.

"Will you go with me, you fine
  lad?
My daughters will wait upon
  you,
My daughters lead off the nightly
  dance,
And cradle and dance and sing you
  to sleep."

Father, father, can you not see
  there
The Erlking's daughters in that dark
  spot?
My son, my son, I see it
  clearly;
The old willows look so grey.

"I love you, your beautiful figure
  charms me;
And if you will not come willingly, I
shall have to use force."
Father, father, now he has hold of
  me!
The Erlking has hurt me!

The father shudders, he rides swiftly
  on,
He holds the moaning child in his
  arms,
He reaches the courtyard with effort
  and distress;
In his arms the child was dead.

# 51

## FRIEDRICH LUDWIG AEMILIUS KUNZEN (1761–1817)
### *Lenore* (1788)

Lenore fuhr ums Morgenrot empor aus schweren Träumen: —

„Bist un - treu, Wil - helm, o - der tot, wie lan - ge willst du sau - men? wie lan - ge willst du säu - men? wie lan - ge? wie lan - ge? wie lan - ge willst du säu-men?"

Er war mit König Friedrichs Macht gezogen in die Prager Schlacht, und hatte nicht

geschrieben: ob er gesund geblieben.

Der König und die Kaiserin,
Des langen Haders müde,
Erweichten ihren harten Sinn
Und machten endlich Friede;
Und jedes Heer mit Sing und Sang,
Mit Paukenschlag und Kling und Klang,
Geschmückt mit grünen Reisern
Zog heim zu seinen Häusern.

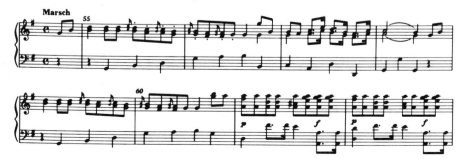

**Marsch**

Und überall, allüberall,
Auf Wegen und auf Stegen,
Zog Alt und Jung dem Jubelschall
Der Kommenden entgegen.
Gottlob! rief Kind und Gattin laut,
Willkommen!-manche frohe Braut.

**Allegro ma non troppo**

aber für Lenoren war Gruß und Kuß verloren.

Sie frug den Zug wohl auf und ab und frug nach allen Namen; doch keiner war, der Kundschaft gab, von allen, so da kamen.

Als nun das Heer vorüber war, zerraufte sie ihr Rabenhaar, und warf sich hin zur Erde mit wütiger Gebärde.

ihn mag ich auf Er - den, mag dort nicht se - lig wer - den."

So wütete Verzweifelung ihr

in Gehirn und Adern. Sie fuhr mit Gottes Führsehung vermessen fort zu hadern; zerschlug den Busen

und zerrang die Hand bis Sonnenuntergang, bis auf am Himmelsbogen die goldnen Sterne zogen.

Und außen horch! ging's trap, trap, trap, als wie von Rosseshufen; und klir-

rend stieg ein Reiter ab an des Geländers Stufen.

Und horch! und horch! den Pfortenring ganz lose, leise

klinglingling! Dann kamen durch die Pforte vernehmlich diese Worte:

und schwang sich auf das Roß behende; wohl um den trauten Reiter schlang

**Più Allegro**

sie ihre Lilienhände, und hurre, hurre, hop, hop, hop! ging's fort in sausendem

Galopp, daß Roß und Reiter schnoben, und Kies und Funken stoben. Zur rechten

und zur linken Hand vorbei vor ihren Blicken, wie flogen Anger, Heid' und Land!

„Graut Lieb - chen auch? Der

Wie donnerten die Brücken!

Mond scheint hell! Hur - ra! Die To - ten rei - ten schnell! Hur-

Rasch auf ein eisern Gittertor
Ging's mit verhängtem Zügel.
Mit schwanker Gert ein Schlag davor
Zersprengte Schloß und Riegel.
Die Flügel flogen klirrend auf,
Und über Gräber ging der Lauf.
Es blinkten Leichensteine
Rund um im Mondenscheine.

Ha sieh! Ha sieh im Augenblick
Huhu! ein gräßlich Wunder!
Des Reiters Koller Stück für Stück
Fiel ab wie mürber Zunder.
Zum Schädel ohne Zopf und Schopf,
Zum nackten Schädel ward sein Kopf;
Sein Körper zum Gerippe
Mit Stundenglas und Hippe.

Hoch bäumte sich, wild schnob der Rapp'
Und sprühte Feuerfunken,
Und hui wars unter ihm hinab
verschwunden und versunken.

Geheul! Geheul aus hoher Luft, Gewinsel kam aus tiefer Gruft.

Lenorens Herz mit Beben, rang zwischen Tod und Leben.

Nun tanzten wohl bei Mondenglanz rund um herum im Kreise die Gei-

„Ge-

ster einen Kettentanz und heulten diese Weise:

-duld! Ge-duld! Wenn's Herz auch bricht! Mit Gott im Him-mel had-re nicht! Des Lei-bes bist du

le-dig; Gott sei der See-le gnä-dig!"

1. Lenore fuhr ums Morgenrot
empor aus schweren Träumen:
"Bist untreu, Wilhelm oder tot,
wie lange willst du säumen?
Er war mit König Friedrichs
    Macht
gezogen in die Prager
    Schlacht,
und hatte nicht geschrieben:
ob er gesund geblieben.

From sickly dream sad Leonor'
upstarts at morning's ray"
"Art faithless William? —or no more?
How long willt bide away?"
He march'd in Fred'rick's war-like
    train,
and fought on Prague's ensanguin'd
    plain;
yet no kind tidings tell,
if William speeds him well.

2. Der König und die Kaiserin,
Des langen Haders müde,
Erweichten ihren harten Sinn
Und machten endlich Friede;
Und jedes Heer mit Sing und Sang,
Mit Paukenschlag und Kling und
    Klang,
Geschmückt mit grünen Reisern
Zog heim zu seinen Häusern.

The king and fair Hungaria's queen
At length bid discord cease;
Each other eye with milder mien,
And hail the grateful peace.
And now the troops, a joyous throng,
With drum and uproar, shout and
    song,
All deck'd in garlands fair,
To welcome home repair.

3. Und überall, allüberall,
Auf Wegen und auf Stegen,
Zog Alt und Jung dem Jubelschall
Der Kommenden entgegen.
Gottlob! rief Kind und Gattin
    laut,
Willkommen! —manche frohe Braut.
Ach! aber für Lenoren
war Gruß und Kuß verloren.

On ev'ry road, on ev'ry way,
As now the crowd appears,
See young and old their path belay,
And greet with friendly tears.
"Praise God!" each child and matron
    cry'd,
And, "Welcome," many a happy bride:
But, ah! for Leonor'
No kiss remains in store!

4. Sie frug den Zug wohl auf und
    ab
und frug nach allen Namen;
doch keiner war, der Kundschaft gab,
von allen, so da kamen.
Als nun das Heer vorüber war,
zerraufte sie ihr Rabenhaar,
und warf sich hin zur Erde
mit wütiger Gebärde.

From rank to rank now see her
    rove,
O'er all the swarming field;
And ask for tidings of her love,
But none could tidings yield.
And when the bootless task was o'er,
Her beauteous ravenlocks she tore;
And low on earth she lay,
And rav'd in wild dismay.

5. Die Mutter lief wohl hin zu ihr:
"Ach daß sich Gott erbarme!
du trautes Kind, was ist mit dir?"
Und schloß sie in die Arme.
"O! Mutter, Mutter! hin ist hin!
Nun fahre Welt und alles hin!
Bei Gott ist kein Erbarmen.
O weh, o weh mir, Armen!"

With eager speed the mother flies:
"God shield us from all harms!
What ails my darling child?" she cries,
And snatch'd her to her arms.
"Ah! mother, see a wretch undone!
What hope for me beneath the sun!
Sure heav'n no pity knows!
Ah! me, what cureless woes!"

6. "Hilf, Gott, hilf! sieh mich gnädig
      an!
Kind, bet' ein Vaterunser!
Was Gott tut, das ist wohl getan!
Gott, Gott erbarmt sich unser!"
"O Mutter, Mutter! eitler Wahn!
Gott hat an mir nicht wohlgetan!
Was half, was half mein Beten?
Nun ist's nicht mehr vonnöten."

"Celestial pow'rs, look gracious
      on!
Haste, daughter, haste to pray'r.
What heav'n ordains is wisely done,
And kind its parent care."
"Ah, mother, mother, idle tales!
Sure heav'n to me no kindness deals.
O, unavailing vows!
What more have I to lose?"

7. "Hilf, Gott, hilf! Wer den Vater
      kennt,
der weiß, er hilft den Kindern.
Das hochgelobte Sakrament
wird deinen Jammer lindern."
"O Mutter, Mutter! was mich brennt,
das lindert mir kein Sakrament!
Kein Sakrament kann Leben
den Toten wiedergeben!"

"O, trust in God! —Who feels
      aright,
Must own his fost'ring care;
And holy sacramental rite,
Shall calm thy wild despair."
"Alas! the pangs my soul invade,
What pow'r of holy rite can aid?
What sacrament retrieve
The dead, and bid them live?"

8. "Hör Kind! Wie, wenn der falsche
      Mann,
im fernen Ungerlande,
sich seines Glaubens abgetan
zum neuen Ehe bande?
Laß fahren, Kind, sein Herz dahin!
er hat es nimmermehr Gewinn!
Wenn Seel' und Leib sich trennen,
wird ihn sein Meineid brennen."

"Perchance, dear child, he loves no
      more;
And, wand'ring far and wide,
Has chang'd his faith on foreign shore,
And weds a foreign bride.
And let him rove and prose untrue!
Ere long his gainless crimes he'll rue.
When soul and body part,
What pangs shall wring his heart!"

9. "O Mutter, Mutter! Hin ist hin!
Verloren ist verloren!
Der Tod, der Tod ist mein Gewinn!
O wär ich nie geboren!
Lisch aus, mein Licht! auf ewig aus!
Stirb hin, stirb hin in Nacht und
      Graus!
Bei Gott ist kein erbarmen
O weh, o weh mir Armen!"

"Ah, mother, mother, gone is gone!
The past shall ne'er return!
Sure death were now a welcome boon:
O had I ne'er been born!
No more I'll bear the hateful light;
Sink, sink, my soul, in endless
      night!
Sure heav'n no pity knows.
Ah! me, what endless woes!"

10. "Hilf, Gott, hilf! Geh nicht ins
      Gericht

"Help, heav'n, nor look with eye
      severe,

mit deinem armen Kinde!
Sie weiß nicht, was die Zunge spricht.
Behalt ihr nicht die Sünde!
Ach, Kind, vergiß dein irdisch Leid
und denk an Gott und Seligkeit!
So wird auch deiner Seelen
der Bräutigam nicht fehlen."

11. "O Mutter! was ist Seligkeit!
O Mutter! was ist Hölle?
Bei ihm, bei ihm ist Seligkeit
und ohne Wilhelm
    Hölle!
Lisch aus, mein Licht, auf ewig aus!
Stirb hin, stirb hin in Nacht und
    Graus!
Ohn' ihn mag ich auf Erden,
mag dort nicht selig werden."

12. So wütete Verzweife-
    lung
ihr in Gehirn und Adern.
Sie fuhr mit Gottes Führsehung
vermessen fort zu hadern;
zerschlug den Busen und zerrang
die Hand bis Sonnenuntergang,
bis auf am Himmelsbogen
die goldnen Sterne zogen.

13. Und außen horch! ging's trap,
    trap, trap,
als wie von Rosseshufen;
und klirend stieg ein Reiter
    ab
an des Geländers Stufen.
Und horch! und horch! den
    Pfortenring
ganz lose, leise klinglingling!
Dann kamen durch die Pforte
vernehmlich diese Worte:

14. "Holla! Holla! tu auf mein Kind!
Schläfst Liebchen oder wachst du?
Wie bist du gegen mich ge-
    sinnt?
Und weinest oder lachst du?"
"Ach, Wilhelm, du? So spät bei
    Nacht?
Geweinet hab' ich und ge-
    wacht;
ach, grosses Leid erlitten!
Wo kommst du her geritten?"

On this deluded maid;
My erring child in pity spare,
She knows not what she said.
Ah! child, all earthly cares resign,
And think of God and joys divine.
A spouse celestial, see—
In heav'n he waits for thee."

"O, mother, what are joys divine?
What hell, dear mother, say?
'Twere heav'n, were dearest William
    mine;
'Tis hell, now he's away.
No more I'll bear the hatefull light:
Sink, sink, my soul, in endless
    night!
All bliss with William flies;
Nor earth, nor heav'n I prize!"

Thus rav'd the maid, and mad
    despair
Shook all her tender frame;
She wail'd at providential care,
And tax'd the heav'ns with blame.
She wrung her hands and beat her breast,
Till parting daylight streak'd the west;
Till brightest starlight shone
Around night's darksome throne.

Now hark! a courser's clatt'ring
    tread,
Alarms the lone retreat;
And straight a horseman slacks his
    speed,
And lights before the gate.
Soft rings the bell; the startl'd
    maid,
Now lists, and lifts her languid head;
When lo, distinct and clear,
These accents reach her ear.

"What, ho! what, ho! ope wide the door!
Speak, love; —dost wake or sleep?
Think'st on me still? —or think'st no
    more?
Dost laugh, dear maid, or weep?"
"Ah! William's voice! so late art
    here?
I've wept and watch'd with sleepless
    care,
And wail'd in bitter woe!
Whence com'st thou mounted so?"

15. "Wir satteln nur um Mitternacht.
Weit ritt ich her von Böhmen.
Ich habe spät mich aufgemacht,
und will dich mit mir nehmen!"
"Ach, Wilhelm erst herein geschwind!
Den Hagedorn durchsaust der
    Wind,
herein, in meinen Armen,
Herzliebster, zu erwarmen!"

"We start at midnight's solemn gloom;
I come, sweet maid, from far.
In haste and late I left my home;
And now I'll take thee there!"
"O, bide one moment first my love,
Chill blows the wind athwart the
    grove;
And here, secure from harm,
These arms my love shall warm."

16. "Laß sausen durch den Hagedorn,
laß sausen, Kind, laß sausen!
Der Rappe scharrt, es klirrt der
    Sporn.
Ich darf allhier nicht hausen.
Komm, schürze, spring' und schwinge
    dich,
auf meinen Rappen hinter mich!
Muss heut noch hundert Meilen
mit dir ins Brautbett eilen."

"Let blow the wind and chill the grove;
Nor wind, nor cold I fear.
Wild stamps my steed; come, haste, my
    love—
I dare not linger here.
Haste, tuck thy coats, make no de-
    lay;
Mount quick behind, for e'en today,
Must ten-score leagues be sped
To reach our bridal bed!"

17. "Ach! wolltest hundert Meilen
    noch
mich heut ins Brautbett' tragen?
Und horch! es brummt die Glocke
    noch,
die elf schon angeschlagen."
"Sieh hin, sieh her! der Mond scheint
    hell.
Wir und die Toten reiten
    schnell.
Ich bringe dich zur Wette,
noch heut' ins Hochzeitbette."

What, ten-score leagues! canst speed
    so far,
Ere morn the day restore?
Hark! hark! the village clock I
    hear—
How late it tells the hour!"
"See there, the moon is bright and
    high,
Swift ride the dead! —we'll bound,
    we'll fly.
I'll wager, love, we'll come,
Ere morn, to bridal home."

18. "Sag an, wo ist dein Kämmerlein?
Wo? Wie dein Hochzeitbettchen?"
"Weit, weit von hier! Still, kühl und
    klein!
Sechs Bretter und zwei Brettchen!"
"Hat's Raum für mich?" "Für dich
    und mich!
Komm, schürze, spring' und schwinge
    dich!
Die Hochzeitgäste hoffen,
die Kammer steht uns offen."

"Say, where is deck'd the bridal hall?
How laid the bridal bed?"
"Far, far from hence, still, cool and
    small;
Six planks my wants bestead."
"Hast room for me?" "For me and
    thee!
Come, mount behind, and hast and
    see
E'en now the bride-mates wait,
And open stands the gate."

19. Schön Liebchen schürzte, sprang
    und schwang
sich auf das Ross behende;
wohl um den trauten Reiter
    schlang

With graceful ease the maiden
    sprung
Upon the coal-black steed,
And round the youth her arms she
    flung,

sie ihre Lilienhände,
und hurre, hurre, hop, hop, hop!
ging's fort in sausendem Galopp,
daß Roß und Reiter schnoben,
und Kies und Funken stoben.

20. Zur rechten und zur linken Hand
vorbei vor ihren Blicken,
wie flogen Anger, Heid' und Land!
Wie donnerten die Brücken!
"Graut Liebchen auch? Der Mond
    scheint hell!
Hurra! Die Toten reiten schnell!
Hurra! Graut Liebchen auch vor
    Toten?"
"Ach nein! doch laß die Toten!"

21. Was klang dort für Gesang und
    Klang?
Was flatterten die Raben?
Horch Glockenklang! Horch
    Totensang:
"Lasst uns den Leib begraben!"
Und näher zog ein Leichenzug,
der Sarg und Totenbahre trug.
Das Lied war zu vergleichen
dem Unkenruf in Teichen.

22. "Nach Mitternacht begrabt den
    Leib,
mit Klang und Sang und Klage!
Jetzt führ ich heim mein junges Weib!
Mit, mit zum Brautgelage!
Komm! Küster, hier! Komm mit dem
    Chor,
und gurgle mir das Brautlied vor!
Komm, Pfaff', und sprich den Segen,
eh' wir zu Bett uns legen!"

23. Still Klang und Sang. Die Bahre
    schwand.
Gehorsam seinem Rufen,
kam's hurre, hurre! nachgerannt
hart hinter's Rappen Hufen;
und immer weiter, hop, hop, hop!
ging's fort in sausendem
    Galopp,
daß Roß und Reiter schnoben,
und Kies und Funken stoben.

And held with fearful heed.
And now they start and speed amain,
Tear up the ground and fire the plain;
And o'er the boundless waste,
Urge on with breathless haste.

Now on the right, now on the left,
As o'er the waste they bound,
How flies the heath! the lake! the clift!
How shakes the hollow ground!
"Art frighted, love? the moon rides
    high.
What, ho! the dead can nimbly fly!
Dost fear the dead, dear
    maid?"
"Ah! no, —why heed the dead!"

Now knell and dirges strike the
    ear;
Now flaps the raven's wing;
And now a sable train ap-
    pear;
Hark! "Dust to dust," they sing.
In solemn march, the sable train
With bier and coffin cross the plain.
Harsh float their accents round;
Like night's sad bird the sound.

"At midnight's hour, the corpse be
    laid
In soft and silent rest!
Now home I take my plighted maid,
To grace the wedding feast!
And, sexton, come with all thy
    train,
And tune for me the bridal strain.
Come, priest, the pray'r bestow,
Ere we to bridebed go!"

The dirges cease—the coffin
    flies,
And mocks the cheated view;
Now rattling dins around him rise,
And hard behind pursue.
And on he darts with quicken'd speed:
How pants the man! —How pants the
    steed!
O'er hill, o'er dale they bound;
How sparkes the flinty ground!

24. Wie flogen rechts, wie flogen links
Gebirge, Bäum' und Hekken!
Wie flogen links und recht und links
die Dörfer, Städt' und Flekken!
"Graut Liebchen auch? Der Mond
    scheint hell!
Hurra! Die Toten reiten schnell!
Graut Liebchen auch vor Toten?"
"Ach laß sie ruhn, die Toten!"

25. Sieh da! sieh da! Am Hochgericht
tanzt, um des Rades Spindel,
halb sichtbarlich, bei Mondenlicht
ein luftiges Gesindel.
"Sasa! Gesindel! Hier! Komm hier!
Gesindel, komm und folge mir!
Tanz' uns den Hochzeitsreigen,
wann wir zu Bette steigen!"

26. Und das Gesindel husch, husch,
    husch!
kam hinten nachgeprasselt,
wie Wirbelwind am Hasel-
    busch
durch dürre Blätter rasselt.
Und weiter, weiter, hop, hop, hop!
ging's fort in sausendem Ga-
    lopp,
daß Roß und Reiter schnoben
und Kies und Funken stoben.

27. Wie flog, was rund der Mond
    beschien,
wie flog es in die Ferne!
wie flogen oben über hin
der Himmel und die Sterne!
"Graut Liebchen auch? Der Mond
    scheint hell!
Hurra! Die Toten reiten schnell!
Graut Liebchen auch vor Toten?"
"O weh! laß ruhn die Toten."

28. "Rapp, Rapp, mich dünkt der
    Hahn schon ruft.
Bald wird der Sand verrinnen—
Rapp, Rapp, ich wittre Morgenluft—
Rapp, tummle dich von hinnen!
Vollbracht, vollbracht ist unser
    Lauf!

On right, on left, how swift the flight
Of mountains woods and downs!
How fly on left, how fly on right,
The hamlets, spires and towns!
"Art frighted, love? —the moon rides
    high.
What ho! the dead can nimbly fly!
Dost fear the dead, dear maid?"
"Ah! leave, ah! leave the dead!"

Lo, where the gibbet scars the sight,
See round the gory wheel,
A shadowy mob, by moon's pale light,
Disport with lightsome heel.
"Ho! hither, rabble, hither come,
And haste with me to bridal home.
There dance in grisly row,
When we to bridebed go."

He spoke, and o'er the cheerless
    waste,
The rustling rabble move:
So sounds the whirlwind's driving
    blast,
Athwart the wither'd grove.
And on he drives with fiercer speed;
How pants the man! how pants the
    steed!
O'er hill and dale they bound;
How sparks the flinty ground!

And all the landscape, far and
    wide,
That 'neath the moon appears;
How swift it flew, as on they glide!
How flew the heav'ns, the stars!
"Art frighted, love? —the moon rides
    high.
What, ho! the dead can nimbly fly!
Dost fear the dead, dear maid?"
"O heav'ns! —Ah! leave the dead!"

"The early cock, methinks I
    hear:
My fated hour is come!
Methinks I scent the morning air:
Come, steed, come haste thee home!
Now ends our toil, now cease our
    cares—

Das Hochzeitbette tut sich auf!
Dit Toten reiten schnelle,
wir sind, wir sind zur Stelle."

29. Rasch auf ein eisen Gittertor
ging's mit verhängtem Zügel.
Mit schwanker Gert ein Schlag
    davor
zersprengte Schloß und Riegel.
Die Flügel flogen klirrend auf,
und über Gräber ging der
    Lauf.
Es blinkten Leichensteine
rund um im Mondenscheine.

30. Ha sieh! Ha sieh im Augenblick,
hu-hu, ein gräßlich Wunder!
Des Reiters Koller, Stück für Stück,
fiel ab wie mürber Zunder.
Zum Schädel ohne Zopf und Schopf,
zum nackten Schädel ward sein Kopf,
sein Körper zum Gerippe
mit Stundenglas und Hippe.

31. Hoch bäumte sich, wild schnob
    der Rapp'
und sprühte Feuerfunken,
und hui! war's unter ihr hinab
verschwunden und versunken.
Geheul! Geheul aus hoher Luft,
Gewinsel kam aus tiefer Gruft.
Lenorens Herz mit Beben,
rang zwischen Tod und Leben.

32. Nun tanzten wohl bei
    Mondenglanz,
rund um herum im Kreise,
die Geister einen Kettentanz,
und heulten diese Weise:
"Geduld! Geduld! Wenns Herz auch
    bricht,
mit Gott im Himmel hadre nicht!
Des Leibes bist du ledig;
Gott sei der Seele gnädig!"

And see, the bridal house appears.
How nimbly glide the dead!
See, here, our course is sped!"

Two folding grates the road belay,
And check his eager speed;
He knocks, the pond'rous bars give
    way,
The loosen'd bolts recede.
The grates unfold with jarring sound;
See, new-made graves bestrew the
    ground,
And tomb-stones faintly gleam,
By moonlight's pallid beam.

And now, O, frightful prodigy!
(As swift as lightning's glare)
The rider's vestments piecemeal fly,
And melt to empty air!
His poll a ghastly death's head shews.
A skeleton his body grows;
His hideous length unfolds,
And sithe and glass he holds!

High rear'd the steed, and sparks of
    fire
From forth his nostrils flew;
He paw'd the ground in frantic ire,
And vanish'd from the view.
Sad howlings fill the regions round;
With groans the hollow caves resound;
And death's cold damps invade
The shudd'ring hapless maid!

And lo, by moonlight's glimm'ring
    ray,
In circling measures hie
The nimble sprites, and as they stray,
In hollow accents cry:
"Though breaks the heart, be mortals
    still;
Nor rail at heav'n's resistless will.
And thou, in dying pray'r,
Call heav's thy soul to spare!"

trans. by Benjamin Beresford (1799)

# 52

GIOVANNI BATTISTA VIOTTI (1755–1824)

*Violin Concerto No. 22 in A Minor (c. 1800),* second movement

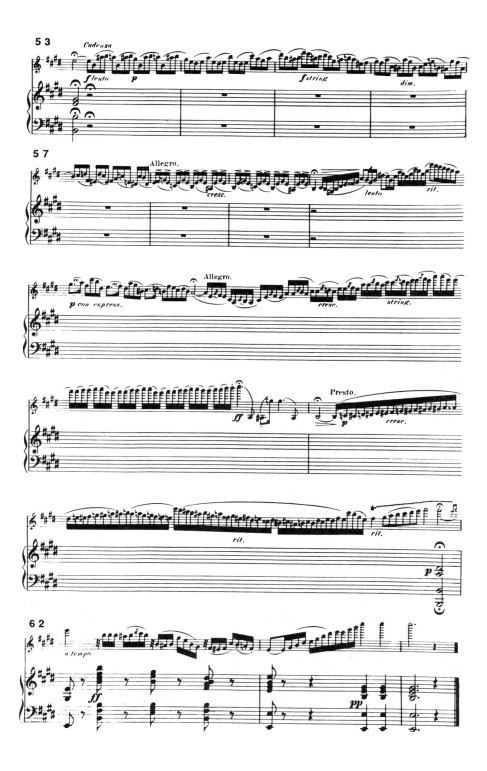

# 53

DANIEL STEIBELT (1765–1823)
*Piano Concerto No. 3*, Op. 33 ("The Storm")
(published 1799), second movement

# 54

## GIOVANNI PAISIELLO (1740–1816)
*Il barbiere di Siviglia* (1782), Act I, trio

**159**

|  |  |
|---|---|
|  | **Svegliato** *(yawning)* |
| Ah! | Ah! |
|  | **Bartolo** |
| Ma dov'eri tu, stordito, | But where were you, idiot . . . |
|  | **Svegliato** |
| Ah! | Ah! |
|  | **Bartolo** |
| allor quando che il Barbiere | when the barber . . . |
|  | **Svegliato** |
| Ah! | Ah! |
|  | **Bartolo** |
| qui s'en venne poco fa? Dov'eri? | went away a short while ago? Where were you? |
|  | **Svegliato** |
| Ah! Io era . . . Ah! Ah! | Ah! I was . . . Ah! Ah! |
|  | **Bartolo** |
| Bravo, bravo, t'ho capito, gran riposta in verità. | Fine, fine. I've understood you; a really great reply. |
|  | **Svegliato** |
| Ah! | Ah! |
|  | **Bartolo** |
| Ma per certo, ci scommetto, qualche astuzia macchinavi. No'l vedesti? | But I'll bet that you were working out some trick. Didn't you see him? |

**Svegliato**

Il vidi . . . ah . . . ah . . . Così male
m'ha trovato, che mi sento, sì
ammalato . . .

I saw him . . . ah . . . ah . . . he
found me so ill, that I now feel much
worse . . .

**Bartolo**

La pazienza perdo già. Dov'e dunque il
Giovinetto? quel briccone dove sta?
Son sicuro in fede mia che v'e qualche
furberia.

I am losing patience. Where then is
Young'un? Where is the rogue? I am
absolutely certain that there is some
trickery going on.

*(Giovinetto comes out an old man, leaning on a cane; sneezes several times.)*

**Svegliato**

Giovinetto . . . vieni qua . . .

Young'un . . . come here . . .

**Giovinetto**

Eccì . . . Eccì . . . Eccì . . .

Achoo . . . Achoo. . . Achoo . . .

**Bartolo**

Via starnuterai domani. Rispondete se
qualcuno da Rosina è qua venuto.

Come on, you can sneeze tomorrow.
Tell me if someone has been here for
Rosina.

**Svegliato**

Ah! . . .

Ah! . . .

**Giovinetto**

Eccì . . .

Achoo . . .

**Bartolo**

Oh che canto è questo qui!

Oh what a business this is!

**Svegliato**

Il bar . . .

The bar . . .

**Bartolo**

Cosa? . . .

What?

**Giovinetto**

Ec . . . Ec . . . Ec . . .

A- A- A-. . .

**Bartolo**

Come? . . . via parlate! Maledetti! non
v'intendo, non comprendo, no, no. Il
Barbiere ci fu, sì, o no?

What? quick, speak!  Cursed fools, I
can't hear you, I don't understand you,
no, no.  Was the barber here or not?

**Svegliato**

Il Barbiere . . . c'è qualcuno?

The barber . . . is that someone?

**Bartolo**

Io scommetto ch'è d'accordo . . .

I'll bet he's his accomplice . . .

**Svegliato**

Io d'accordo . . .

Me . . . accomplice?

**Giovinetto**

| | |
|---|---|
| Non signore . . . c'e giustizia . . . | Ah no, sir.  There's such a thing as justice . . . |

**Bartolo**

| | |
|---|---|
| Che giustizia . . . son padrone ed ho ragion . . . | What justice . . . I am the boss and I am right . . . |

**Giovinetto**

| | |
|---|---|
| Ma s'è ver . . . | But if it is true . . . |

**Bartolo**

| | |
|---|---|
| Non vo'che sia. | I do not wish it to be true. |

**Svegliato**

| | |
|---|---|
| Dunque è meglio d'andar via . . . | Then we had better quit . . . |

**Bartolo**

| | |
|---|---|
| Certo meglio assai sarà. | Yes, indeed, that would be much the best . . . |

**Giovinetto**

| | |
|---|---|
| Dunque è meglio d'andar via . . . | Then we had better quit . . . |

**Bartolo**

| | |
|---|---|
| Certo meglio assai sarà. | Yes, that would be much the best. |
| | *(imitating them)* |
| Chi stranuta, chi  sbadiglia . . . lungi andate cento miglia. | One sneezes at me, the other yawns . . . Go a hundred miles away. |

**Giovinetto and Svegliato** *(sniveling)*

| | |
|---|---|
| Se non fosse la signora. | If it were not for the signora. |

**Bartolo**

| | |
|---|---|
| Dunque andate alla buon'ora. | So be sure to leave straightaway. |

**Giovinetto and Svegliato**

| | |
|---|---|
| no, nessun starebbe qua | No, no one would stay here. |

**Bartolo**

| | |
|---|---|
| e partite via di qua. | Clear out at once. |

*(The servants leave.)*

# 55

PAISIELLO

*Il barbiere di Siviglia*, Act I, Rosina's *cavatina*

Giusto ciel, chi conoscete
quanto il cor onesto sia,
deh voi date all'alma mia,
quella pace che no ha.

Just heaven, who knows
How pure is my heart,
I pray you to give to my soul
That peace that I do not have.

# 56

## HAYDN
*Piano Sonata in C Major,* Hob. XVI:48 (1789), first movement

# 57

HAYDN
*Piano Trio in C Minor*, Hob. XV:13 (1789),
second movement

# 58

HAYDN
*String Quartet in Bb Major*, Opus 33, No. 4,
Hob. III:40 (1781), first movement

# 59

HAYDN
*String Quartet in C Major*, Opus 54, No. 2,
Hob. III:57 (1788), second movement

# 60

HAYDN
*Piano Sonata in E♭ Major*, Hob. XVI:52 (1794),
first and second movements

# 61

HAYDN
*String Quartet in G Major*, Opus 77, No. 1,
Hob. III:81 (1799), second movement

# 62

## MOZART
*Piano Sonata No. 14 in C Minor, K.457 (1784),*
first movement

# 63

## MOZART
*String Quintet in E♭ Major, K.614 (1791), second movement*

*Neue Mozart Ausgabe*, Serie VIII, Werkgruppe 19, Abteilung 1, ed. by Ernst Hess and Ernst Fritz Schmid. © 1967 by Bärenreiter-Verlag, Kassel. All Rights Reserved. Reprinted by Permission.

# 64

MOZART
*Symphony No. 41 in C Major* ("Jupiter"), K.551
(1788), fourth movement

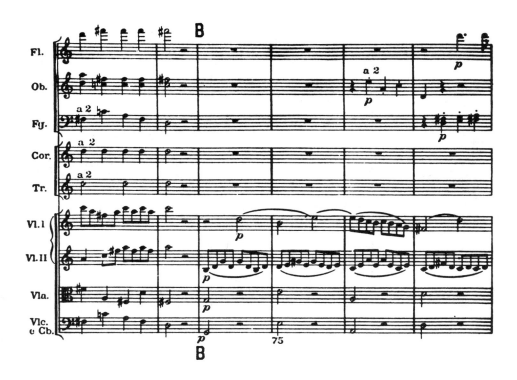

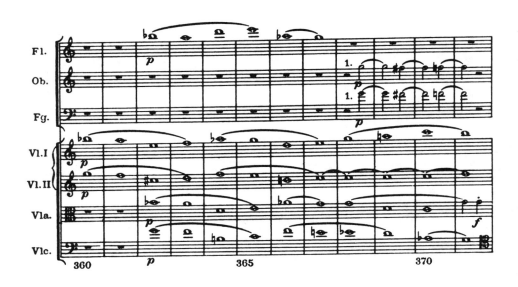

390

395

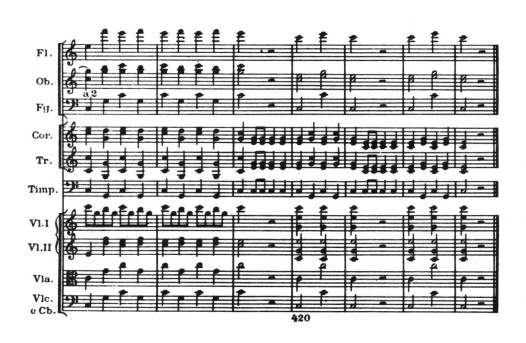

# 65

## MOZART
*Minuet No. 2 in C Major, K.601 (1791)*

*Neue Mozart Ausgabe*, Serie IV, Werkgruppe 13, Abteilung 1, Band 2, ed. by Marius Flothuis. © 1988 by Bärenreiter-Verlag, Kassel. All Rights Reserved. Reprinted by Permission.

# 66

MOZART
*Le nozze di Figaro,* K.492 (1786), Act II, Scene
1: "Porgi amor"

# 67

MOZART
*Die Zauberflöte*, K.620 (1791), Act I, Finale

Fünfzehnter Auftritt
DIE DREI KNABEN führen TAMINO herein, jeder hat einen silbernen Palmzweig in der Hand.

**Nr. 8 Finale**
**Larghetto**

(Er geht an die Pforte rechts, macht sie auf, und als er hinein will, hört man von fern eine Stimme.)

mir noch nicht er-laubt. Er-klär' dies Rät-sel, täusch mich nicht.    Die Zunge

bindet Eid und Pflicht. Wann al-so wird die Dek-ke schwinden?    So-

bald dich führt der Freundschaft Hand ins Hei-lig-tum zum ew'-gen Band.

O ew'ge Nacht! wann wirst du schwinden? Wann wird das Licht mein Auge

### Achtzehnter Auftritt

Ein Zug von Gefolge; zuletzt fährt SARASTRO auf einem Triumphwagen heraus,
der von sechs Löwen gezogen wird. Vorige.

bedecket ih_re Häupter dann, sie müs_sen erst ge _ rei _ nigt sein.

(Zwei bringen eine Art Sack und bedecken *damit* die Häupter *von TAMINO und PAPAGENO.)*

CHOR
Sopran/Alt

Wenn Tugend und Ge_rechtigkeit     der Gro_ßen

Tenor

Wenn Tugend und Ge_rechtigkeit     der Gro_ßen

Baß

Wenn Tugend und Ge_rechtigkeit     der Gro_ßen

Presto

Pfad mit Ruhm be _ streut, der Gro_ßen     Pfad mit Ruhm be _ streut, mit Ruhm be_

Pfad mit Ruhm be _ streut, der Gro_ßen     Pfad mit Ruhm be _ streut, mit Ruhm be_

Pfad mit Ruhm be _ streut, der Gro_ßen     Pfad mit Ruhm be _ streut, mit Ruhm be_

## Scene 15

*(The Three Boys lead Tamino on. Each has a silver palm frond in his hand.)*

### Three Boys

| | |
|---|---|
| Zum Ziele führt dich diese Bahn, | This road will lead you to your goal, |
| doch mußt du, Jüngling, männlich siegen. | Yet must you, youth, conquer like a man. |
| Drum höre unsre Lehre an: | And so listen to our teachings: |
| Sei standhaft, duldsam und verschwiegen! | Be constant, be tolerant, and be discreet. |

### Tamino

| | |
|---|---|
| Ihr holden Kleinen, saget an, | Dear little boys, tell me |
| ob ich Paminen retten kann? | Whether I shall be able to rescue Pamina. |

### Three Boys

| | |
|---|---|
| Dies kund zu tun, steht uns nicht an— | This information is not for us to give— |
| sei standhaft, duldsam und verschwiegen— | Be constant, be tolerant, and be discreet— |
| bedenke dies; kurz, sei ein Mann! | Bethink yourself of these; in short, be a man! |
| Dann, Jüngling, wirst du männlich siegen. | Then, youth, you will, as a man, be victorious. |

*(They go off.)*

### Tamino

| | |
|---|---|
| Die Weisheitslehre dieser Knaben | May the wise teachings of these boys |
| sei ewig mir ins Herz gegraben. | Be ever engraved on my heart. |
| Wo bin ich nun? Was wird mit mir? | Where am I now? What is going to happen to me? |
| Ist dies der Sitz der Götter hier? | Is this the dwelling place of the Gods? |
| Doch zeigen die Pforten, es zeigen die Säulen, | But the doors and the columns show |

| | |
|---|---|
| daß Klugheit und Arbeit und Künste hier weilen; | That Prudence, and Work and Art live here; |
| wo Tätigkeit thronet und Müßiggang weicht, | Where Activity reigns and Idleness is weak, |
| erhält seine Herrschaft das Laster nicht leicht. | Vice finds it difficult to dominate. |
| Ich wage mich mutig zur Pforte hinein, | I'll wager I have the courage to go in this door, |
| die Absicht ist edel und lauter und rein. | My intention is honorable, clear, and pure. |
| Erzittre, feiger Bösewicht! | Tremble, cowardly villain! |
| Paminen retten, Paminen retten ist mir Pflicht. | To rescue Pamina, to rescue Pamina is my duty. |

*(He goes to the right-hand door, opens it, and as he is about to enter, we hear a voice from far off.)*

**Voice**

| | |
|---|---|
| Zurück! | Go back! |

**Tamino**

| | |
|---|---|
| Zurück? zurück? | Go back? Go back? |
| So wag' ich hier mein Glück! | Then I'll try my luck here! |

*(He goes to the door on the left.)*

**Voice** *(from inside)*

| | |
|---|---|
| Zurück! | Go back! |

**Tamino**

| | |
|---|---|
| Auch hier ruft man zurück? | They are telling me to go back, here as well? |

*(He looks around.)*

| | |
|---|---|
| Da seh' ich noch eine Tür! | I see one other door! |
| vielleicht find' ich den Eingang hier. | Perhaps I'll gain an entrance here. |

*(He knocks on the middle door; an elderly Priest appears.)*

**Priest**

| | |
|---|---|
| Wo willst du, kühner Fremdling, hin? | What do you want here, audacious stranger? |
| was suchst du hier im Heiligtum? | What are you looking for in this sanctuary? |

**Tamino**

| | |
|---|---|
| Der Lieb' und Tugend Eigentum. | I seek Love and Virtue. |

**Priest**

| | |
|---|---|
| Die Worte sind von hohem Sinn! | The words have a fine ring to them! |
| Allein, wie willst du diese finden? | But how do you propose to find them? |
| Dich leitet Lieb' und Tugend nicht, | Love and Virtue are not your guides, |
| weil Tod und Rache dich entzünden. | For you are fired by thoughts of Death and Revenge. |

**Tamino**

| | |
|---|---|
| Nur Rache für den Bösewicht. | Revenge only for the villain. |

**Priest**

| | |
|---|---|
| Den wirst du wohl bei uns nicht finden. | You won't find any such here among us. |

**Tamino**

| | |
|---|---|
| Sarastro herrscht in diesen Gründen? | Does Sarastro rule in these parts? |

**Priest**

| | |
|---|---|
| Ja, ja! Sarastro herrschet hier. | Yes, indeed! Sarastro rules here. |

**Tamino**

| | |
|---|---|
| Doch in der Weisheit Tempel nicht? | But not in the Temple of Wisdom? |

**Priest** (*slowly*)

| | |
|---|---|
| Er herrscht im Weisheitstempel hier. | He rules here in the Temple of Wisdom. |

**Tamino** (*starts to leave*)

| | |
|---|---|
| So ist denn alles Heuche-lei! | So then everything has been a pack of lies. |

**Priest**

| | |
|---|---|
| Willst du schon wieder gehn? | Are you going already? |

**Tamino**

| | |
|---|---|
| Ja, ich will gehen froh und frei, nie euren Tempel sehn. | Yes, I will go away, happy and free, Never to see your Temple. |

**Priest**

| | |
|---|---|
| Erklär dich näher mir, dich täuschet ein Betrug. | Tell me more, You have been deceived somehow. |

**Tamino**

| | |
|---|---|
| Sarastro wohnet hier, Das ist mir schon genug. | Sarastro lives here, And that is quite enough for me. |

**Priest**

| | |
|---|---|
| Wenn du dein Leben liebst, so rede, bleibe da! Sarastro hassest du? | If you love your life Stay there, and speak. Do you hate Sarastro? |

**Tamino**

| | |
|---|---|
| Ich haß' ihn ewig, ja! | Yes, I hate him for eternity! |

**Priest**

| | |
|---|---|
| Nun gib mir deine Gründe an! | Give me your grounds |

**Tamino**

| | |
|---|---|
| Er ist ein Unmensch, ein Tyrann! | He is inhuman, a tyrant! |

**Priest**

| | |
|---|---|
| Ist das, was du gesagt, erwiesen? | Are you sure of what you say? |

**Tamino**

| | |
|---|---|
| Durch ein unglücklich Weib bewiesen, | I have it from an unfortunate woman, |
| das Gram und Jammer niederdrückt. | Cast down by sadness and misery. |

**Priest**

| | |
|---|---|
| Ein Weib hat also dich berückt? | So, a woman has captivated you? |
| Ein Weib tut wenig, plaudert viel. | A woman does very little and talks a lot. |
| Du, Jüngling, glaubst dem Zungenspiel? | Do you, young man, believe everything you are told? |
| O legte doch Sarastro dir | O were Sarastro to tell you |
| die Absicht seiner Handlung für! | The purpose of his actions! |

**Tamino**

| | |
|---|---|
| Die Absicht ist nur allzu klar; | The purpose is all too clear to me: |
| riß nicht der Räuber ohn' Erbarmen | Did not the robber mercilessly tear |
| Paminen aus der Mutter Armen? | Pamina from her mother's arms? |

**Priest**

| | |
|---|---|
| Ja, Jüngling, was du sagst, ist wahr. | Yes, young man, what you say is true. |

**Tamino**

| | |
|---|---|
| Wo ist sie, die er uns geraubt? | Where is she, whom he stole from us? |
| Man opferte vielleicht sie schon? | Is she already sacrificed? |

**Priest**

| | |
|---|---|
| Dir dies zu sagen, teurer Sohn, | Dear son, to tell you about it |
| ist jetzund mir noch nicht erlaubt. | Is not possible at this time. |

**Tamino**

| | |
|---|---|
| Erklär' dies Rätsel, täusch' mir nicht. | Answer this riddle, don't deceive me. |

**Priest**

| | |
|---|---|
| Die Zunge bindet Eid und Pflicht. | Duty and oath bind my tongue. |

**Tamino**

| | |
|---|---|
| Wann also wird die Decke schwinden? | And when will this blanket of obscurity be lifted? |

**Priest**

| | |
|---|---|
| So bald dich führt der Freundschaft Hand | As soon as the hand of friendship guides you |
| ins Heiligtum zum ew'gen Band. | Into the sanctuary to the eternal brotherhood. |

*(He goes off.)*

**Tamino**

| | |
|---|---|
| O ew'ge Nacht! wann wirst du schwinden? | O everlasting night! when will dawn break? |
| Wann wirst das Licht mein Auge finden? | When will the light reach my eyes? |

**Chorus** *(offstage)*

| | |
|---|---|
| Bald, bald, Jüngling, oder nie! | Soon, soon, youth, or never! |

### Tamino

| | |
|---|---|
| Bald, bald, bald sagt ihr, oder nie! | Soon, soon, soon you say, or never! |
| Ihr Unsichtbaren, saget mir | You invisible ones, tell me |
| Lebt denn Pamina noch? | Is Pamina still alive? |

### Chorus *(offstage)*

| | |
|---|---|
| Pamina, Pamina, lebet noch! | Pamina, Pamina still lives! |

### Tamino *(joyfully)*

| | |
|---|---|
| Sie lebt? sie lebt? | She lives? She lives? |
| Ich danke euch dafür | I thank you for that |

*(He takes out his flute.)*

| | |
|---|---|
| O wenn ich doch imstande wäre | O if only I could |
| Allmächtige, zu eurer Ehre | Almighty ones, in your honor, |
| mit jedem Tone meinen Dank zu | Depict my thanks with every |
| schildern, | sound |
| wie er hier, *(auf Herz deutend)* | As it springs *(indicating his heart)* |
| hier entsprang. | from here. |

*(He plays on his flute. Wild animals of all kinds come out to listen to him.*
*He stops and they run away. The birds sing an accompaniment.)*

| | |
|---|---|
| Wie stark ist nicht dein Zauberton! | How powerful is your magic sound, |
| weil, holde Flöte, durch dein Spielen | Dear flute, for through your playing |
| selbst wilde Tiere Freude fühlen. | Even wild animals feel happiness |

*(He plays.)*

| | |
|---|---|
| Doch nur Pamina bleibt davon. *(spielt)* | Yet only Pamina stays aloof. *(he plays)* |
| Pamina, höre mich! *(spielt)* | Pamina, listen to me! *(he plays)* |
| Umsonst, umsonst! *(spielt)* | It's no use, no use! *(he plays)* |
| Wo? *(spielt)* Ach, wo, wo find ich | Where? *(he plays)* Ah, where shall I |
| dich? | find you? |

*(Papageno answers offstage with his little pipes.)*

| | |
|---|---|
| Ha! das ist Papagenos Ton. | Ha! That's the sound of Papageno. |

*(He plays—Papageno answers—he plays—Papageno answers.)*

| | |
|---|---|
| Vielleicht sah er Paminen schon! | Perhaps he has already seen Pamina! |
| Vielleicht eilt sie mit ihm | Perhaps she is hurrying to me with |
| zu mir! | him! |
| Vielleicht führt mich der Ton zu ihr. | Perhaps the sound will lead me to her. |

*(He hurries off.)*

### Scene 16

*(Papageno and Pamina hurry in.)*

### Papageno, Pamina

| | |
|---|---|
| Schnelle Füße, rascher Mut, | Speedy feet and stout heart |
| schützt vor Feindes List und | Protect us from the treachery and rage |
| Wut; | of the enemy |
| fänden wir Tamino doch, | Let us now find Tamino, |
| sonst erwischen sie uns noch! | or they'll soon catch us. |

### Pamina

| | |
|---|---|
| Holder Jüngling! | Dear lad! |

**Papageno**

Stille, stille, ich kann's besser.                    Quiet, quiet, I know a better way

*(He pipes—Tamino answers—he pipes—Tamino answers.)*

**Papageno, Pamina**

Welch Freude ist wohl größer,          What joy could be greater,
Freund Tamino hört uns schon;          Our friend Tamino hears us already;
hieher kam der Flötenton!              The sound of his flute came this way!
Welch ein Glück, wenn ich ihn finde;    What happiness if I could find him;
nur geschwinde, nur geschwinde!        Quickly, let us hurry!

*(They start to leave.)*

**Monostatos** *(mocking them)*

Nur geschwinde, nur geschwinde!        Quickly, let us hurry!


**Scene 17**
**Monostatos and the above**

**Monostatos**

Ha! hab' ich euch noch erwischt!       Ha! now at last I've got you!
Nur herbei mit Stahl und Eisen!        Come here with the steel and iron!
Wart', man wird euch Mores Weisen!     Wait a bit, you'll learn how to behave!
Den Monostatos berücken!               Try to deceive Monostatos, would you!
Nur herbei mit Band und Stricken!      Bring up the ropes and cords!
He, ihr Sklaven, kommt herbei!         Hey, you slaves, come on here!

**Pamina, Papageno**

Ach, nun ist's mit uns vorbei!         Ah, now it's all over for us.

**Monostatos**

He, ihr Sklaven, kommt herbei!         Hey, you slaves, come along!

*(The slaves enter with fetters.)*

**Papageno**

Wer viel wagt, gewinnt oft viel,       He who bets high often wins big.
komm, du schönes Glockenspiel,         Come you beautiful glockenspiel
laß die Glöckchen klingen, klingen,    Let your little bells ring-a-ding
daß die Ohren ihnen singen.            And make their ears sing-along.

*(Papageno plays on his glockenspiel. Monostatos and the slaves dance.)*

**Monostatos, Chorus of Slaves**

Das klinget so herrlich,               It sounds so lovely
das klinget so schön!                  It sounds so sweet
Larala, larala.                        Larala, larala.
Nie hab' ich so etwas                  Never have I heard or seen
gehört und gesehn!                     Anything like this!

*(They go marching off.)*

Larala, larala                         Larala,  larala

### Pamina, Papageno *(laughing)*

| | |
|---|---|
| Könnte jeder brave Mann | If only every brave man |
| solche Glöckchen finden, | Could find such little bells, |
| seine Feinde würden dann | Then his enemies |
| ohne Mühe schwinden, | Would disappear without difficulty, |
| und er lebte ohne sie | And without them he would live |
| in der besten Harmonie. | In sweetest harmony. |
| Nur der Freundschaft Harmonie | Only the concord of friendship |
| mildert die Beschwerden; | Overcomes hardships; |
| ohne diese Sympathie | And without this sympathy |
| ist kein Glück auf Erden. | There is no happiness on earth. |

### Chorus *(offstage)*

| | |
|---|---|
| Es lebe Sarastro, Sarastro lebe! | Long live Sarastro, long live Sarastro! |

### Papageno

| | |
|---|---|
| Was soll das bedeuten? | What does that mean? |
| Ich zittre, ich bebe. | I'm trembling, I'm shivering. |

### Pamina

| | |
|---|---|
| O Freund, nun ist's um uns getan! | O my friend! Now it's all over for us! |
| dies kündigt den Sarastro an. | That announces Sarastro. |

### Papageno

| | |
|---|---|
| O wär' ich eine Maus, | Oh, if only I were a mouse, |
| wie wollt' ich mich verstecken, | How I would hide myself! |
| wär' ich so klein wie Schnecken, | If I were like a snail, |
| so kröch' ich in mein Haus. | I'd creep into my house. |
| Mein Kind, was werden wir nun | My child, what shall we say |
| sprechen? | now? |

### Pamina

| | |
|---|---|
| Die Wahrheit! die Wahrheit! | The truth! The truth! |
| sei sie auch Verbrechen. | Even though it may confess wrong-doing. |

## Scene 18
### A procession of followers; at the end comes Sarastro on a triumphal chariot, drawn by six lions. Characters as above.

### Chorus
*(Sarastro gets down from the chariot during the chorus.)*

| | |
|---|---|
| Es lebe Sarastro, Sarastro soll leben! | Long live Sarastro, may Sarastro live long! |
| Er ist es, dem wir uns mit Freuden ergeben! | It is he to whom we joyfully submit ourselves! |
| Stets mög' er des Lebens als Weiser sich freu'n. | May he, wise as he is, always enjoy life. |
| Er ist unser Abgott, dem alle sich weih'n. | He is our idol, to whom we all dedicate ourselves. |

**Pamina** *(kneels)*

Herr! ich bin zwar Verbrecherin!
ich wollte deiner Macht entflieh'n,
allein die Schuld ist nicht an mir—
der böse Mohr verlangte Liebe;
darum, o Herr, entfloh ich dir.

Lord! I have truly offended!
I wished to flee from your realm,
But the fault is not entirely mine—
The wicked Moor demanded my love
So, Lord, I ran away from you.

**Sarastro**

Steh auf, erheitre dich, o Liebe!
denn ohne erst in dich zu dringen,
weiss ich von deinem Herzen mehr:
Du liebest einen andern sehr.
Zur Liebe will ich dich nicht zwingen,
doch geb' ich dir die Freiheit nicht.

Stand up, my dear, and be cheerful!
For without even having to press you,
I know more about your feelings:
You love another very deeply.
I shall not force you to love,
Yet neither shall I give you your
    freedom.

**Pamina**

Mich rufet ja die Kindespflicht,
denn meine Mutter—

My filial duty calls me,
For my mother—

**Sarastro**

Steht in meiner Macht;
du würdest um dein Glück gebracht,
wenn ich dich ihren Händen ließe.

—is in my power;
Your happiness would be at an end
Were I to leave you in her hands.

**Pamina**

Mir klingt der Mutter Namen
    süße:
sie ist es—

The name "Mother" sounds so sweet
    to me:
And she is that—

**Sarastro**

Und ein stolzes Weib.
Ein Mann muß eure Herzen leiten;
denn ohne ihn pflegt jedes
    Weib
aus ihrem Wirkungskreis zu
    schreiten.

—and a proud woman.
A man has to guide your hearts;
For without him, every woman
    habitually
Steps outside her proper sphere.

### Scene 19
### Monostatos, Tamino. The above.

**Monostatos**

Na, stolzer Jüngling, nur
    hieher,
hier ist Sarastro, unser Herr.

Now, arrogant young fellow, come
    along,
Here is Sarastro, our master.

**Pamina**

Er ist's!

It's he!

**Tamino**

Sie ist's!

It's she!

**Pamina**

| | |
|---|---|
| Ich glaub' es kaum! | I can hardly believe it! |

**Tamino**

| | |
|---|---|
| Sie ist's! | It's she! |

**Pamina**

| | |
|---|---|
| Er ist's! | It's he! |

**Tamino**

| | |
|---|---|
| Es ist kein Traum! | This is no dream! |

**Pamina**

| | |
|---|---|
| Es schling' mein Arm sich um ihn her. | I'll put my arm around him. |

**Tamino**

| | |
|---|---|
| Es schling' mein Arm sich um sie her, | I'll put my arm around her, |

**Pamina, Tamino** *(they embrace)*

| | |
|---|---|
| und wenn es auch mein Ende wär'. | Even if I had to die for it! |

**Chorus**

| | |
|---|---|
| Was soll das heissen? | What's all this? |

**Monostatos**

| | |
|---|---|
| Welch eine Dreistigkeit! | The impudence! |
| Gleich auseinander, | Break it up, there! |
| das geht zu weit! | This is going too far! |

*(He parts them—kneels.)*

| | |
|---|---|
| Dein Sklave liegt zu deinen Füßen, | Your slave lies at your feet, |
| laß den verweg'nen Frevler büßen. | Let the audacious criminal suffer. |
| Bedenk', wie frech der Knabe ist! | Just think how impudent the lad is! |

*(pointing to Papageno)*

| | |
|---|---|
| Durch dieses seltnen Vogels List | Through the trickery of this singular bird |
| wollt' er Paminen dir ent-führen; | He wanted to steal Pamina away from you; |
| allein ich wußt' ihn aufzu-spüren. | However, I knew how to track him down. |
| Du kennst mich! meine Wachsamkeit— | You know me. My watchfulness— |

**Sarastro**

| | |
|---|---|
| Verdient, daß man ihr Lorbeer streut! | —deserves to be covered with laurels! |
| He! gebt dem Ehrenmann sogleich— | Here! Give this honored man imme-diately— |

**Monostatos**

| | |
|---|---|
| Schon deine Gnade macht mich reich. | Your grace already makes me rich. |

**Sarastro**

| | |
|---|---|
| Nur siebenundsiebzig Sohlenstreich. | Just seventy-seven blows on his feet. |

**Monostatos**

Ach Herr! den Lohn verhofft' ich nicht.

Oh, Lord! I didn't look for such a reward.

**Sarastro**

Nicht Dank! Es ist ja meine Pflicht.

No gratitude! I only do my duty.

*(Monstatos is led away.)*

**Chorus**

Es lebe Sarastro, der göttliche Weise,
er lohnet und strafet in ähnlichem Kreise.

Long live Sarastro. In his godly wisdom
He rewards and punishes at the same time.

**Sarastro**

Führt diese beiden Fremdlinge
in unsern Prüfungstempel ein,
bedecket ihre Häupter dann,
sie müssen erst gereinigt sein.

Take both these strangers
Into our testing temple,
Let their heads be covered,
They must first be purified.

*(Two people bring a kind of sack and with them cover the heads of Tamino and Papageno.)*

**Chorus**

Wenn Tugend und Gerechtigkeit
der Großen Pfad mit Ruhm bestreut,
dann ist die Erd' ein Himmelreich,
und Sterbliche den Göttern gleich.

When Virtue and Justice
Bestrew the path of the great ones with fame
Then is the earth a realm of heaven,
And mortals are like the Gods themselves.

# 68

## MOZART
*Ave verum corpus*, K.618 (1791)

*Neue Mozart Ausgabe*, Serie I, Band 3, ed. by Helmut Federhofer. © 1963 by Bärenreiter-Verlag, Kassel. All Rights Reserved. Reprinted by Permission.

Ave, verum corpus, natum de Maria
   virgine;
Vere passum, immolatum in cruce pro
   homine;
Cujus latus perforatum unda fluxit et
   sanguine.
Esto nobis praegustatum in mortis
   examine.

Hail, true body, born of the Virgin
   Mary;
Who truly suffered, sacrificed on the
   Cross for mankind;
From whose pierced side flowed water
   and blood.
Be a foretaste for us of the trial of
   death.

# 69

LUDWIG VAN BEETHOVEN (1770–1827)
*Piano Sonata in F Minor*, Opus 2, No. 1 (1795),
first movement

# 70

BEETHOVEN
*Piano Sonata in C Major* ("Waldstein"), Opus 53
(1804), first and second movements

# 71

BEETHOVEN
*Andante favori* for piano, WoO 57 (1803)

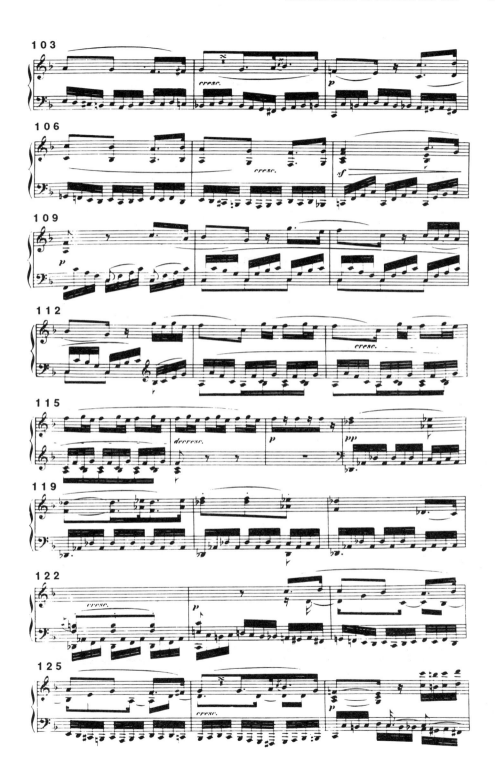

# 72

BEETHOVEN
*Piano Sonata in E Major*, Opus 109 (1820)

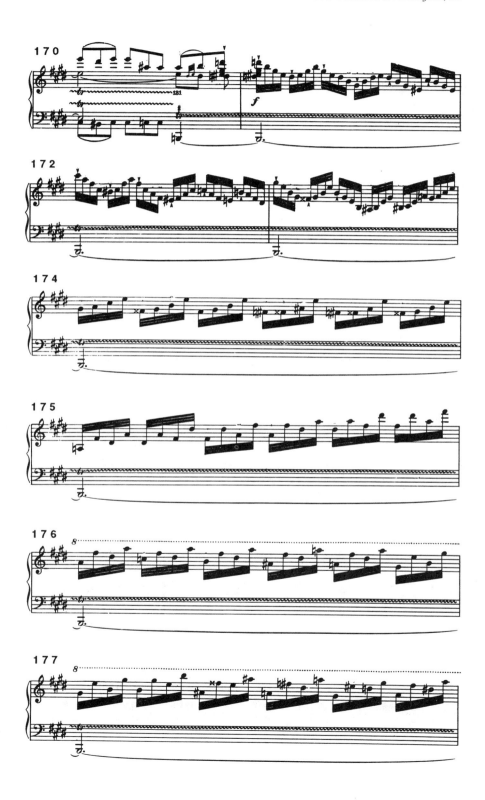

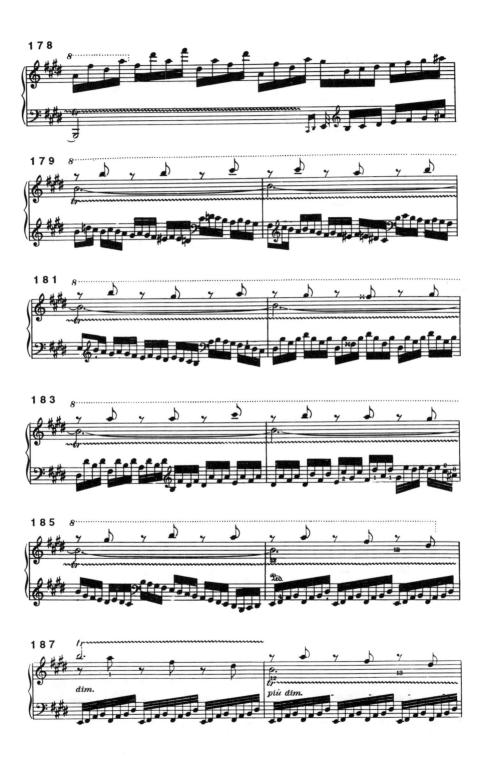

# 73

BEETHOVEN
*Symphony No. 9*, Opus 125 (1824), first
movement

**196**

**231**

**239**

**3 5 7**

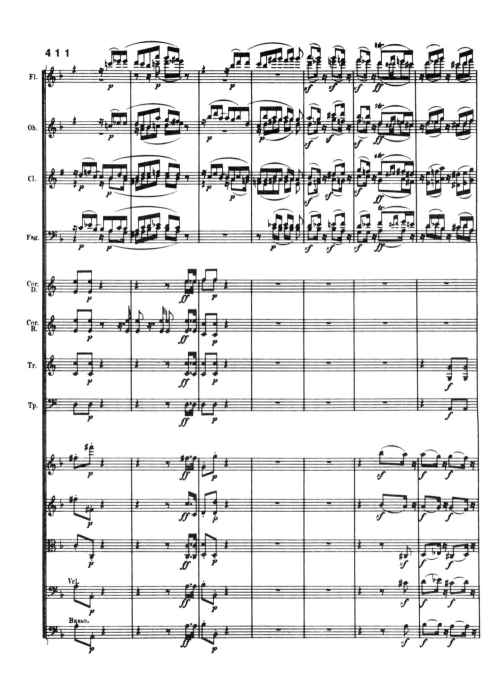

**5 3 4**

# 74

CLEMENTI
*Piano Sonata in A Major*, Opus 50, No. 1
(1821), second movement

# 75

**JOHN FIELD (1782–1827)**
*Piano Concerto No. 2 in A♭ Major* (published 1814), first movement

# 76

## GIOACCHINO ROSSINI (1792–1868)
## *Il barbiere di Siviglia* (1816), Act I, No. 7: Duet

**118**

R. lar,_____ che_ mi_ de - vi_ con - so - lar, sì, con - so -
star,_____ My_ de - light, my_ shin - ing_ star, my shin - ing

F. nar? chi v'ar - ri - va, chi v'ar - ri - va a indo - vi - nar, a in - do - vi -
are! What a puz-zle, What a puz-zle wom-en are! Too sly by

**121**

R. lar, sì, con - so - lar, sì, con-so - lar!
star, my shin - ing star, my shin-ing star!

(Figaro leaves)

F. nar, a in - do - - vi - nar, a in-do -vi - nar?
far! Too sly by far! Too sly by far!

*ff*

# Appendix

## GLOSSARY OF TERMS IN THE SCORES

This glossary includes only terms found in this anthology. One common form of a word is given ("legato"); the reader can easily deduce the meaning of its variations ("ligato"). Omitted are foreign terms very similar to English ones ("espressione," "spirito") or in common use ("solo").

*a.* To, at, with
*adagio.* Slowly, leisurely
*affetuoso.* Tenderly
*allegretto.* A moderately fast tempo
*allegro (all°).* A rapid tempo (between allegretto and presto)
*andante.* A moderately slow tempo (between adagio and allegretto)
*andantino.* A tempo usually played faster than andante
*appena sentit.* Hardly audible
*assai.* Very
*attacca.* Go on to the next movement without a break

*ben.* Very
*brio.* Vigor and spirit

*cantabile.* In a singing style
*choeur.* Chorus
*col cante.* Accompaniment should follow the singer
*colla parte.* Accompaniment should follow the main part
*col' 8va.* Doubled at the octave below (lit. "with the octave")
*come.* As, like
*con.* With

*cominciando a diminuire sino alla fine.* Diminishing until the end
*crescendo (cres., cresc.).* Becoming louder
*cresc. il fr.* Grow louder to forte

*da capo.* Repeat from the beginning
*decrescendo (decresc.).* Becoming softer
*diminuendo (dim.).* Becoming softer
*dolce (dol.).* Sweet, gentle

*eco.* Echo
*espressivo.* Expressive
*etwas langsamer als das Thema.* A little slower than the theme
*fine.* End
*forte (f., for., fr.).* Loud
*fortissimo (ff., frmo.).* Very loud
*fortississimo (fff.).* Extremely loud
*forte piano (fp.).* Loud, then immediately soft

*Gesangvoll, mit innigster Empfindung.* Melodious, with heartfelt emotion
*grave.* Heavy, strong
*grazioso.* Graceful

*larghetto.* Somewhat faster than largo
*largo.* A very slow tempo

*largo con moto.* Somewhat faster than largo

*legato.* Smooth

*leggiermente.* Lightly

*lento.* A slow tempo (between andante and largo)

*loco.* At notated pitch

*ma.* But

*maestoso.* Majestic

*mässig langsam.* Moderately slowly

*marcato.* With emphasis

*meno.* Less

*mezza voce (m.v.).* Only moderately loud (lit. "half-voice")

*mezzo.* Moderately

*moderato.* At a moderate tempo

*molto.* Very much

*morendo.* Dying away

*moto.* Motion

*m.s.* Play with left hand

*ohne Flügel.* Without harpsichord

*ped.* Use pedal

*pianissimo (pianiss., pp.).* Very soft

*pianississimo (ppp.).* Extremely soft

*piano (p., pia., po.).* Soft

*più.* More

*pizzicato (pizz.).* Plucked (the string plucked by the finger)

*poco.* Little

*poco a poco.* Little by little

*prestissimo.* Faster than presto

*presto.* A very quick tempo (faster than allegro)

*rallentando.* Becoming slower

*recitativo (recit.).* A singing style imitating speech

*rinforzando (r., rf., rinf., rinforzato).* Emphasis on a note or chord

*ritardando (ritard.).* Slowing

*ritournelle.* Repeated section

*scherzando, scherzoso.* Playfully

*sciolte.* Unconstrained; in a free manner

*secco.* Dry

*sehr lebhaft und schauerlich.* Very quickly and with horror

*sempre.* Always

*senza.* Without

*sforzando (sf., sfz., forz., ffz., fz.).* With sudden emphasis

*sfp.* With sudden emphasis, then immediately soft

*sine diminuendo, senza diminuendo (sin. d., sin. dim.).* Without getting softer

*Singstimme.* Voice part

*smorzando (smorz.).* Dying away

*sostenuto.* Sustained

*sotto voce.* In an undertone

*spiccato.* Detached (bow is dropped on the string and is lifted again after each note)

*spiritoso.* Spirited

*stringend (string.).* Quickening

*subito.* Suddenly

*sul una corda.* With the soft pedal (lit. "on one string")

*tanto.* So much

*tasto solo (tasto).* No accompaniment other than the bass note (lit. "solo fingering")

*teneramente.* Tenderly, gently

*tenuto (ten.).* Held, sustained

*tr.* Trill

*troppo.* Too much

*tutti.* All

*tutti le corde.* No soft pedal (lit. "all the strings")

*unis.* Unison

*vivace, vivo.* Lively